"We will rebu
and we will be st
and we will be in it

PAT OWENS, Grand Forks mayor

A SEA OF ROOFTOPS

Water still reaches the rooftops of houses in the Lincoln Drive neighborhood of Grand Forks on April 28, more than a week after the flood. Only 27 of the roughly 2,500 single-family homes in East Grand Forks were untouched by floodwaters.

J. ALBERT DIAZ

We found strength in a shared nightmare

Winter was the hardest in memory. And spring the cruelest.

The blizzards began before Thanksgiving and ended after Easter with Hannah, the meanest of all – a storm with the force of an Atlantic hurricane and the cold of an arctic night.

But the blizzards were only a prologue to the nightmare that overtook the Red River Valley. Hard on the heels of hard-hearted Hannah, the Red River delivered its record flood.

The twin cities of Grand Forks and East Grand Forks bore the brunt of both winter and water.

Then came fire. Much of the historic heart of Grand Forks was burned away.

It was an unprecedented catastrophe, and the Grand Forks Herald was here to cover it. The Herald has served the Red River Valley for more than a century. Its staff lived with the winter, reporting every day on conditions throughout the valley. When the flood came, we were joined by journalists who work for other newspapers that are owned by Knight-Ridder Inc. When the fire struck, we continued to publish. The best of our work is in this book.

For our cities, the Flood of 1997 has been a defining moment. Much has been lost. Nothing will be quite the same. While the water found its level in our homes and businesses, we found strength in our community and in ourselves.

Here is the story of our community's heroic fight against the elements and of eventual victory. This is a story that all of us in the region experienced. This is a story that strangers came to share.

It is an inspiring story.

This book is dedicated to those who lived through the winter and the flood, who fought the flood and the fire, who came to our cities to help and to those who will live in our rebuilt cities.

A part of the proceeds from sales of this book will help build a bigger, better, stronger community.

Mike Jacobs

Mike Jacobs, editor

Michael Maidenberg

Michael Maidenberg, publisher

Come Hell
and
High Water

By the staff of the Grand Forks Herald and Knight-Ridder Newspapers
Writer: **Ryan Bakken**
Editor: **Mike Jacobs**
Book design: **Steve Rice**
Picture editors: **John Stennes** and **Bill Alkofer**
Research: **Erik Siemers**
Artists: **Lee Hulteng** and **Greg Harmel**
Technical editors: **Dave Bacig** and **Mike Bulger**

Fourth Printing: **January 1998**

Library of Congress Cataloging-in-Progress.
Come Hell and High Water, photographs by the staff of the Grand Forks Herald and Knight-Ridder Newspapers; editing by Mike Jacobs, picture editing by Steve Rice and Bill Alkofer.

p. cm.
ISBN 0-9642860-2-5
(pbk.) : $14.95

A portion of the profits from this book will go to flood-relief efforts.

A HELPING HAND
(PREVIOUS PAGE)
Bob Bushy steadies the hand of his daughter's friend Karen Bockwitz as she leaves Bushy's East Grand Forks home on May 2.

JOHN STENNES

A FIREFIGHTER'S FUTILE EFFORT
(RIGHT)
Grand Forks firefighter Mike Sande struggles through 38-degree floodwater to attach a hose to a submerged hydrant. The April 19 downtown fire rages behind him.

BILL ALKOFER

UNITED AGAIN
Cars stream over the Kennedy Bridge after it opened to traffic at 8:10 a.m. Monday, April 28 — 10 days after flooding closed it. The bridge was the first link between the two cities.

J. ALBERT DIAZ

The worst of times, the best of people

First came the snow. Then the ice. Then the river. And then the river of tears.

They weren't all tears of grief, fright and despair. For every teardrop of sorrow that streamed down our cheeks, three fell because of the pride we felt in our fight, because we found that the worst of times brought out the best in people and because we were dramatically reminded of what's really important in our lives.

The water found its level, and that level invaded our homes, our security and our future, changing us and our community forever.

But the water also took us to new levels — of strength, compassion, resolve and caring — that we may not have known we could reach. In that way, too, it changed us and our community forever.

The water ran deep at 54.11 feet. But its depth didn't match the depth of our spirit. In East Grand Forks and Grand Forks and isolated areas north and south — the river ran through it.

"Whatever doesn't kill us makes us stronger," the saying goes.

Our sacrifice for that strength was great. Our future is as murky as the chocolate floodwaters that held hostage our community for two weeks. And we haven't felt the last of our pain.

The property losses are measurable in terms of dollars. But the real hurt comes when we calculate the time, effort and sacrifice required to accumulate those items lost. But, as flood victim after flood victim came to realize: "Those are only things." Or, "It's just stuff."

But there was still a sense of betrayal hard to shake because we're taught that hard work is the elixir of success. Work hard enough, and everything will be fine.

That had been the way it was with the Red and Red Lake rivers. We'd lost a skirmish or two to them over the years, but the wars were always won. When the water lapped at our dikes, we rolled up our sleeves. When the water receded, we rolled them back down and continued to regard the channel as our friendly foe.

We returned to normal.

The winter of 1996-97 wasn't normal. Not remotely close. Even old-timers noted for their "remember when" stories

EARLY EFFORTS
Volunteers from the Point area form a human chain to build a sandbag dike in East Grand Forks on April 12.
JOHN STENNES

*"We fought this thing.
We fought it all night long.
We fought and fought
and fought."*

MARY ANDERSON, East Grand Forks resident

IN THE TRENCHES
Red River Valley volunteers work to the last wisps of light while fighting the flood on Drayton's Main Street. The efforts paid off, as the city held off floodwaters.

DAVID P. GILKEY

"We're all each other's neighbors, especially when we're dealing with the forces of nature."

TOM MULHERN,
United Way

pronounced it the worst in their substantial memories. Grand Forks had a record snowfall of 98.6 inches. A record eight blizzards turned us into hostages in our own homes. The last of them was also a record-breaker — for cruelty.

When we survived Blizzard Hannah's power that knocked out our power, we thought we'd weathered the climatic disaster of a lifetime.

We were correct — for two weeks. Then came another record-breaker in what was called the Flood of the Century. Or any century, at least as many as we remember.

Then, a fire claimed all or parts of 11 downtown Grand Forks buildings that stood in four feet of water. Ice and now fire. And water everywhere, but not a drop fit to douse the blaze. The community's feelings of hopelessness had crested.

It was in this context that Herald staffer Andy Braford twisted a popular phrase to create the headline "Come hell and high

water" for the April 21 Herald edition produced by the flood- and fire-displaced newspaper's staff.

Hell and high water indeed. But the headline had a second meaning — that no matter what disaster would befall us next, the fight would continue. The headline became a popular phrase among flood victims, accentuating their determination in the wake of months of events that could have crushed it.

In the end, we realized that dogged preparation, backbreaking work and shoulder-to-shoulder persistence were no match for the forces of nature.

We lost to the river, if you use dikes topped, basements ruined and neighbors homeless as your scoreboard.

If you measure battles by how nobly they were fought or by the human spirit they reveal, then we are winners.

Left in the ashes and silt of hell and high water, we prevailed.

—————

Ryan Bakken

LOVE AMONG LOSSES
Connie and Roger Srnsky embrace on May 24 in what once was the dining room of their home in East Grand Forks' Sherlock Park.
CANDACE BARBOT

The blizzards hit and hit and hit ...

STUCK

A motorist uses his car door as a shield on Dec. 17 as Blizzard Betty's blustery 40-mph winds and 50-below wind chill blasted the region. Betty was the second of a record eight blizzards to hit the Red River Valley in a season.

DAN DIEDRICH

Before becoming the Fertile police chief, Pat Tuseth was a medical examiner for Polk County.

"I was involved on the bad side of these things then, on the ones where it was too late," Tuseth said.

In the early hours of Jan. 11, Tuseth and Minnesota State Trooper Bob Norland were just early enough.

They pulled Fertile resident Shane Schmitz from his pickup stuck in a snowdrift on a rural dirt road. Visibility was near zero, so Norland had to run ahead of the Blazer as a guide. Winds gusted to 35 mph and the wind chill was 50 below.

After four hours stuck in a snowdrift, Schmitz had hypothermia, with a core temperature of 94, and carbon monoxide poisoning.

"With another one or two degrees of temperature, in combination with the carbon monoxide, you don't come to again," Tuseth said. "The doctor said that another 20 minutes and we wouldn't have gotten him back."

Schmitz is back, as healthy as ever. "I'm just loving life because now I can watch Cody, my 2-year-old son, grow up," Schmitz said. "The more I look at it every day, the more lucky I feel."

Others were not as fortunate. Four people from the three-state area, including two within a 100-mile radius of Fertile, died during the three-day blizzard of Jan. 9-11 that

spared Shane Schmitz. Just about every blizzard claimed a life in some way.

UND student Francis Delabreau died trying to walk two miles back to his dorm room in Blizzard Andy, the winter's first, on Nov. 17. His body was not found until Jan. 4, frozen in an abandoned

struck the region, bringing life to a standstill.

Grand Forks received a record 98.6 inches of snowfall. The previous record was 89.1 inches in 1897, the year the Red River reached its previous record crest.

To the south, there was even more snow and even more snowmelt headed

and wind chills of 50 below were common throughout the winter.

■ Life disrupted: Interstate 29 was closed on 18 days and U.S. Highway 2 on 17 days because of low visibility and snowplowing ... School was canceled — six days in Grand Forks, seven days in East Grand Forks and even more in rural areas such as Thompson, N.D., where 13 days were lost to the weather... Collapsed roofs... Streets so narrow and with snow piled so high that drivers felt they were going through tunnels... Snowdrifts that reached to the top of roofs and overpasses.

FRANZI FRUSTRATES TRAVELERS

Snowplow drivers work to free two tractor-trailers from ditches along Interstate 29 northbound near Thompson, N.D., on Jan. 22, during Blizzard Franzi. Blowing snow created near-zero visibility, closing the interstate for much of the day.

CHUCK KIMMERLE

van.

It was a brutal winter not just for lives lost to blizzards. It also brought the snowfall that became snowmelt that became the Flood of the Century. And it was a killer psychologically, as people began to feel like prisoners in their homes.

The winter started savagely. And it grew worse. "We've already had a month of January weather, and January isn't even here yet," Leon Osborne of UND's Regional Weather, Information Center said on Dec. 18.

Andy was not the exception, but rather the rule, as eight blizzards

north. Fargo had 117 inches, 28 more than its previous record.

But the winter brought more than snow.

■ The cold: November's average temperature was 9.4 degrees below normal, and December and January also were significantly colder than average. There was no midwinter thaw to provide relief; the temperature climbed above freezing only one day in December and three in January.

■ The wind: While Blizzard Elmo dropped less than an inch of snow, it produced gusts to 50 mph and wind chills to 70 below. Gusts of 30 mph

The weather didn't even cooperate when it was nice. Two warm and sunny days to begin 1997 reduced the First Night ice sculptures in downtown Grand Forks to puddles.

Nice weather was rarely the problem. After Doris delivered its blow in early January, Dennis Walaker, manager of operations for Fargo Public Works, suggested that everyone look on the bright side. "There's only 86 days 'til April," he said.

But April didn't end the misery.

TRUDGING THROUGH DRIFTS

Irene DeVos, 82, struggles down a path in Lyon County, Minn., cut in a 20-foot-high snowdrift during Blizzard Elmo on Jan. 15. Elmo didn't drop much snow but brought wind chills of 70 below.

BILL ALKOFER

THE EIGHT BLIZZARDS

		SNOWFALL	ACCUMULATED
ANDY	NOV. 16-17	12 IN.	13.6 IN.
BETTY	DEC.16-18	8.7 IN.	38.2 IN.
CHRISTOPHER	DEC. 20	4.2 IN.	42.4 IN.
DORIS	JAN. 9-11	8.8 IN.	56.5 IN.
ELMO	JAN. 14-16	0.4 IN.	57.1 IN.
FRANZI	JAN. 22-23	8.6 IN.	67.4 IN.
GUST	MARCH 4	0.2 IN.	83.3 IN.
HANNAH	APRIL 4-6	6.3 IN.	97.4 IN.

TOTAL: **98.6 INCHES**

Blizzard: Wind speeds of 35 mph or more, considerable falling and/or drifting snow, visibility near zero.

BILL ALKOFER

BLUSTERY WINDS
Tim Holt takes a breather while digging out after Blizzard Elmo. The blizzard hit on Jan.14 with devastating winds of 50 mph.

Hannah cruelest of all

Blizzard Hannah was frightening. Scott Lind and his 13-year-old daughter Brandie were trapped inside their pickup between downed power lines, one wire settled on the hood, another snagged behind the cab. Leaving the cab risked electrocution, so they spent 45 harrowing minutes until rescuers arrived to free them from the high-voltage fence.

Blizzard Hannah was deadly. Its victims included Troy Swartz of Lankin, N.D., who froze to death after his car became stuck in the snow on a rural road.

Blizzard Hannah was an adventure. Because they had no power, Jill and Paul Anderson of Hillsboro, N.D., pitched a tent in their living room for both warmth and entertainment — as a camping experience.

Blizzard Hannah was a gigantic disruption. The five members of the Beth and Kyle Grove family of rural East Grand Forks spent several days in the warmth of the shelter at the Grand Forks Civic Auditorium. They were among an estimated 300,000 people who lost power, some for a week, in an area that ran roughly from the Canadian border 160 miles to the south and 40 miles on both sides of the Red River.

Blizzard Hannah was devastating. Ada, Minn., farmer Kenny Visser couldn't prevent about 20 cattle and 40 hogs from drowning in floodwaters that accompanied Hannah. The livestock remained

HANNAH'S HIGH TOLL

Livestock farmer Kenny Visser of Ada, Minn., lost about 20 cattle and 40 hogs in the frozen floodwaters. Visser crouches next to one of his cattle on April 10, after the Wild Rice River flooded his farm and then froze during Blizzard Hannah.

BILL ALKOFER

grotesquely frozen in ice a week later.

Blizzard Hannah was many things to many people. She also was many forces of nature. Rain, ice, snow, wind, cold and, ultimately, flood.

Standing alone, Hannah was a climatic event of a lifetime. She reached the highest category of blizzard issued by the National Weather Service and had hurricane-strength winds. One of the most intense storms in decades, the weather experts said.

Her devastation wasn't complete during her three-day stay. The additional moisture provided the final punch to the flood knockout.

Hannah began with rain on April 4, a Friday. That turned to freezing rain, the ice causing power lines to droop. Wind whipped the lines like playground swings. Poles snapped like match sticks. More than 2,000 poles fell in the valley, meaning long hours for linemen.

"It took 35 years to build this system, and Mother Nature took it apart in a couple of hours," said Mike McMahon, general manager of the Red River Valley Rural Electric Cooperative.

Seven inches of blinding snow followed, leaving people without heat, lights, power, cable TV. No comfort. Nowhere to go.

Families huddled in blankets around fire-places and battery-operated radios. Life's everyday conveniences, long taken for granted, became luxuries.

Even more than robbing electrical power, Hannah stole personal power. Two national sports championships for UND and a steady snowmelt had provided comfort for residents worn thin from a winter of isolation, frustration and fear. But Hannah provided one final, relentless reminder of the worst winter in history ...

... that soon became the worst flood in history.

"*I've been
praying a lot.
One minute I pray
for a miracle,
the next I pray
to God to help me
understand why
this is happening.*"

KENNY VISSER,
Ada, Minn., farmer

**SNAPPED LIKE
TOOTHPICKS**
Rural power
lines in Norman
County, Minn., lie
in ruins after
Blizzard Hannah
coated them with
ice and leveled
them with winds
of 44 mph. More
than 300,000
people were
without power,
some for more
than a week.
BILL ALKOFER

SLIPPED THROUGH THE CRACKS
Mike Babler slips through a layer of ice into knee-deep water in Ada, Minn., on April 8. Most of the town was evacuated when floodwaters raged into town and then froze after Blizzard Hannah.

BILL ALKOFER

AN ICY BORDER

Ice hangs from a sign along the Marsh River in Minnesota's Norman County on April 12. The state line between Minnesota and North Dakota was defined by ice and the swollen Red River of the North.

BILL ALKOFER

NO GAS, LOTS OF WATER (RIGHT)

Roger Gilberg reaches out of his garage on April 16 to pull in a boat, piloted by Arven Mayer, that ran out of gas in Breckenridge, Minn. Floodwaters in Breckenridge forced 1,000 of the city's 3,700 residents to evacuate and damaged 500 buildings.

BILL ALKOFER

AIRBORNE THAW

A North Dakota National Guard helicopter dumps sand on ice covering the Red River north of Grand Forks on March 31. It was the largest "ice dusting" operation in the state's history, an effort to use the sun's thermal energy to speed up thawing, thus preventing ice jams on the river.

JOHN STENNES

A wicked winter springs a muddy wall of water

As she was being evacuated from her home in Breckenridge, Minn., Beth Meyer spoke for many in the Red River Valley. "We call this the winter from hell," she said.

In Breckenridge and in Ada, Minn., hell froze over.

Breckenridge and Ada took on a lunar look when the flood froze, leaving jagged sheets of dirty blond ice in the streets. "It looked like a photograph of a lake with whitecaps," Ada Mayor Russ Onstad remembers.

Every community in the Red River basin endured blizzards and floods. Fate delivered them simultaneously in Ada and Breckenridge. The moment gripped the nation's attention. President Clinton said television footage of sandbaggers working through the blizzard helped him realize the area's plight.

Breckenridge not only suffered a double disaster the weekend of April 4-6, it sustained two hits of flooding with 500 buildings damaged and evacuation of 1,000 of its 3,700 residents.

The Red River is born in Breckenridge, where the Bois de Sioux and Otter Tail rivers meet. Overland flooding from the Otter Tail River swamped north Breckenridge on April 5.

RIVER RESCUERS
Dave Shockley, left, is evacuated from his Breckenridge house by boat in the evening hours of April 15, after Kirk Peterson, center, and Errow Hensch rescued him.

CAROLYN KASTER

Nine days later, it was worse. The overflowing Bois de Sioux put more than five feet of water on south Breckenridge streets. Residents were evacuated just ahead of the tide. The next day, trapped inside the dike with nowhere to drain and in temperatures near zero, the water froze.

"They took our floodwater out in gravel trucks," said Jack Thompson, Wilkin County emergency manager.

The Breckenridge evacuees included Lonnie and Debbie Pierce and their three children. Jena, 8, Donald, 6, and Dillon, 2, clung to their mother in the pitch black of a National Guard troop carrier escaping the danger.

"Mama, I'm scared and I'm cold and it's dark," Jena said. With a reassuring hug, Debbie answered, "There's nothing to be scared of. We're all safe."

Safe, but not sound. "I've had three strokes and colon cancer, but this is something very different," said 79-year-old Margaret Olson, who was carried out of a nursing home on a National Guardsman's back.

During the first crest, Vice President Al Gore visited Breckenridge. When the second crest came, residents were looking for more than political help. "Forget vice presidents; the pope should come next time," Jackie

Peterson said. "We need divine intervention."

In Ada, an ice jam on the Wild Rice River carved up a levee on April 6, sending a two-foot wall of water through the town. Water invaded 90 percent of the homes in the town

> **"Mama,
> I'm scared and
> I'm cold and
> it's dark."**
>
> JENA PIERCE,
> Breckenridge, Minn.

LEAVING IN A HURRY

National Guardsman Conrad Anderson lifts Dorothy Pierce, 77, into a waiting truck early on April 15, as Breckenridge floodwaters continue to rise. Pierce's daughter-in-law, Debbie Pierce, follows, carrying her son Dillon to the truck. Evacuations were hurried as more than five feet of water covered south Breckenridge.

Top, the family waits for a ride out of the troubled area.

CAROLYN KASTER (TOP)
BILL ALKOFER (BOTTOM)

A REST EARNED
Pam Cizek takes a break from sandbagging in front of her Breckenridge home on April 16.
BILL ALKOFER

A WALK IN ICY WATER
Sam Neubauer wades along a street near his Breckenridge home with groceries and clothing he retrieved from his flooded house on April 15. Wilkin County Sheriff's Deputy Mike Gaulrappe patrols for other residents searching for a ride.
CAROLYN KASTER

BASEMENT WADING
Chris Rosenau, 19, sorts through what's left of his basement bedroom in Ada, Minn., on April 9.
BILL ALKOFER

Red River Valley Chronology

NOVEMBER

16-17 — Blizzard Andy dumps 12 inches of snow, leaving two dead in a car crash near Greenbush, Minn.

DECEMBER

3 — Grand Forks voters approve the Aurora events center with 53 percent of vote.

16-18 — Blizzard Betty arrives five days before winter officially starts.

20 — Blizzard Christopher, the second blizzard in a week, drops 4.2 inches of snow.

25 — Temperatures plunge to 40 below at Flag Island on Lake of the Woods, setting a record for Minnesota's coldest Christmas.

30 — Four people die when a tracked van plunges through Lake of the Woods.

31 — Thousands participate in the third annual First Night celebration in downtown Grand Forks.

JANUARY

4 — The body of 26-year-old UND student Francis Delabreau, missing since the Nov. 17 blizzard, is found frozen in an abandoned van.

9-11 — Blizzard Doris takes four lives as wind chills reach 80 below.

11 — The National Guard is activated to clear snow-blocked roadways.

12 — President Clinton declares the region a disaster area, clearing money for storm costs.

WAITING AMIDST FLOODWATERS

With a scarf protecting her new hairdo, Fredda Larson waits with water at her feet to be evacuated from the York Manor Residence, a Breckenridge home for the elderly, as floodwaters rise in the residence's community room on April 15.

CAROLYN KASTER

of 1,700 people.

With power knocked out the day before by the ice storm and the water too deep for even four-wheel drive vehicles to escape, residents sat in dark, cold, water-logged homes until National Guard trucks arrived from Moorhead. When all but a few evacuated, Ada became an ice-caked ghost town.

"Everything bad that could possibly be imagined has happened," Mayor Onstad said.

In Ada, as in Breckenridge, streets were cleared by chopping the ice into chunks and hauling the flood away.

Unlike its neighbors along the Red, Fargo, the valley's biggest city, was spared a major blow. It had only about 40 homes with major damage — but there were dramatic moments. Officials said the city narrowly escaped inundation.

"We spent a lot of money being lucky," Fargo city engineer Mark Bittner said.

WAITING AND WATCHING

A herd of deer, above, is stranded on what has become an island in the flooded Red River Valley near Hendrum, Minn. Grain farmer Jay Tommerdahl, 23, left, watches the Wild Rice River as it advances on his barn.

BILL ALKOFER

AN ICY, SUGARY GLAZE

A field lies frozen in floodwater from the Red and Wild Rice rivers near Perley, Minn. Sugar beet growers estimated the late planting would mean a setback of $5.5 million.

CAROLYN KASTER

Ready, but not for 54 feet

Pat and Margo Svoboda's garage has been flood control headquarters for Riverside Park since 1989.

It's a convenient location; their home at 101 Park Avenue is just a few strides from the dike that protects the north end of the neighborhood. In flood times, the garage was supplied with food, portable toilets, radio and telephone communications, couches for volunteers before and after their dike-walking shifts, even cable television. It was also the neighborhood's social hangout when the Red River threatened.

"This year we were really ready," Pat said. "We were in that garage laughing at the flood. Fifty feet? Hey, bring it on. We were ready. I guess we shouldn't have been laughing."

Riverside's dikes were beefed up. Mounds of extra clay — small mountains, really — were at the ready. Grand Forks and East Grand Forks had never been better prepared. Officials drew on lessons learned in 1979, when the Red River hit its highest point so far this century. There were detailed flood-fighting plans. With contingencies. Dikes were raised throughout the cities.

DEVASTATION ON LINCOLN DRIVE

About 8 feet of water covers the Lincoln Drive area on April 18. Homes here were evacuated hours before the dikes gave way.

JACKIE LORENTZ

> ## *"I don't lose battles that can be won by hard work. But 52 feet was as high as we could go."*
>
> **DICK OLSON,** Grand Forks resident

JANUARY

14-16 — Blizzard Elmo arrives, prompting Minnesota Gov. Arne Carlson to close all Minnesota schools.
15 — The U.S. Army Corps of Engineers unveils $40 million ring levee proposal that would protect Grand Forks from a 100-year flood.
22-23 — Blizzard No. 6 is Franzi.

FEBRUARY

2 — A Northwest Airlines DC-9 skids off an icy runway at Grand Forks International Airport.
14 — The National Weather Service's first outlook on Grand Forks flooding says the river may rise higher than 1979's crest of 48.8 feet.
28 — The National Weather Service gives flood forecast of 47.5 - 49 feet at Grand Forks.

MARCH

1 — Grand Forks Red River defeats Grand Forks Central 2-1 for its second straight state high school hockey title.
4 — Blizzard Gust adds to the record snowfall, causing the roof of the East Grand Forks Civic Center to sag.

22 — At home, the UND women's basketball team wins the school's first NCAA Division II title by defeating Southern Indiana 94-78.
28 — The National Weather Service sticks to its forecast of 47.5 - 49 feet.

END OF A FUTILE FIGHT
Kathy LaVoi sits on the dike around her home in the Burke Addition south of Grand Forks on April 18. About a foot of water was in the basement by noon, and LaVoi couldn't keep up.

CHUCK KIMMERLE

Sandbags were standing by. A diversion was in place to handle the English Coulee, which soaked so much of the city 18 years earlier.

The cities laughed at 50 feet. And at 51. But when the water reached 52 feet, laughter turned to tears. The river won.

Half an hour before midnight on April 18, the Svobodas shared their sorrow with their son Ryan, who is 16. For two weeks, Ryan and his buddies had hoisted sandbags every waking moment when they weren't in school. They were among legions of volunteers of all ages, from all walks of life, from near and far, from groups too numerous to name or thank, who worked around the clock, often at the sacrifice of their own property.

"As a parent, it was hard to see your son cry, especially since he's usually not an emotional kid," Margo said. "Those poor kids — they'd worked so hard and came up with nothing."

The Svoboda family's sobbing group hug came a few minutes after someone from the U.S. Army Corps of Engineers pulled the plug on a giant pump and said, "We're done. Folks, you've done your best. It's time to leave."

Just past dawn the next day, Riverside Park was surrounded. Water came from the south via the sewers. Water poured over the dike behind Riverside Pool, just like a waterfall. When the water

BREACHING OF HOPES
Water pours over dikes in the Lincoln Drive area on April 18. By 2:30 p.m., water had poured down every street in the neighborhood, and water was halfway up the houses' walls.

BILL ALKOFER

reached its level, it left $90,000 in damage in the Svoboda home.

Just before Pat left, as the water swirled around

his house, he placed a cross across a window ledge. "Our tears were about all the effort, not our possessions," he said.

REMNANTS OF A WAR ZONE

A Humvee rolls through the empty, powerless downtown area of Grand Forks. The downtown area remained without power for more than a month.

J. ALBERT DIAZ

"It's Vietnam all over again. Hueys in the air. You eat what you can when you can... camouflage all over."

MIKE FLANNERY,
Grand Forks police officer and Vietnam War veteran

MARCH

29 — UND wins its sixth NCAA Division I hockey championship by defeating Boston University 6-4 in Milwaukee.

APRIL

3 — Sandbagging and dike-building begin in Greater Grand Forks.

4 — Grand Forks Emergency Manager Jim Campbell issues an urgent call for sandbag volunteers to raise dikes three to seven feet at Riverside Park.

4 — Blizzard Hannah arrives with freezing rain that will leave 300,000 valley residents without power.

4 — Red River reaches 28-foot flood stage.

5 — Wind and ice knock down KXJB-TV's 2,060-foot transmitter near Galesburg, N.D.

5 — At Breckenridge, Minn., sandbagging goes on despite the blizzard. Floodwaters force hundreds from the city.

5 — The National Weather Service sticks to its 49-foot crest prediction despite precipitation from Blizzard Hannah.

7 — The Red River rises to 38.27 feet. National Weather Service still says 49 feet.

7 — For the second time this year, President Clinton

"If it had been about possessions, we'd have moved everything out a week before."

But that effort wasn't rendered meaningless. "No, you can't say the effort was wasted because we lost," Margo said. "When the flood comes, you all band together. Everyone's equal. That's quite a feeling.

"You do what you can to help your neighbors because you know they'd help you."

The power of the water moved freezers and dislodged houses from their foundations. But when the Svobodas returned to their home to survey the damage, the cross was still on the window ledge.

DIFFERENT WINTER, DIFFERENT MELT

The Red River's spring ascent has always been stately. Slowly and surely the Red has risen along its 565-mile route from Breckenridge to Lake Winnipeg, its crest levels and dates becoming more predictable as the flooding headed north.

But 1997 was different, tragically different. Just like the winter.

This year, the Red rose fast and furiously. It left its neighbors no time to prepare, much less to rest. Two feet a day — an inch an hour — the river rose day after day, going higher even when the wisdom of riverwatchers, lay and scientific alike, suggested that its rise would slow.

Portions of the sister cities already were underwater — and the rest under siege — by the time the accurate prediction of 54 feet came. By then, it was too late.

Too late to prevent more than an estimated $1 billion damage to the two

EARLY MORNING EVACUATIONS

Grand Forks firefighters Stewart Chase, left, and Bob Karel carry a resident of the Ryan House through the flooded lobby of the senior citizens apartment building on April 19. Firefighters and the Coast Guard began moving the building's residents at 4 a.m. as the city continued its evacuation.

BILL ALKOFER

cities alone. Too late to prevent water from entering about 11,000 homes and businesses in Grand Forks and all but 27 single-family residences in East Grand Forks.

Too late to stop 50,000 residents of the two cities from fleeing their homes like refugees in a war-torn country. Too late to stop the ruin of businesses and the loss of jobs. Too late to stop the hurt to hearts, to souls, to plans and dreams. Just too late.

The Red and its sibling, the Red Lake River, didn't single out properties with river views. The streams also ravaged what had before been considered untouchable turf.

When the Red cut a wider channel through the two cities that weekend in

mid-April, it twisted land-scapes and lives.

They were landscapes and lives already bent by what might have been the hardest winter ever. The water, of course, was the result of a record snowfall. When that snowfall was trumped with a crippling Blizzard Hannah and a week of cold, the experts were left baffled.

Five days before the water escaped its normal channel, the National Weather Service was sticking to a 49-foot crest forecast. Then the prediction went up five times in five days, the most dramatic increase coming after the water had become unstoppable.

The changing forecasts took an emotional toll. "People were warned to have certain expectations, and when those expectations have been shattered again and again, they get skeptical," Tim Lamb of Grand Forks said. "They ought to be willing to say, 'We just don't know what to expect,' instead of throwing us these incremental things. It's driving us up the wall."

"Mother Nature threw us a curve," said Dean Braatz, hydrologist at the North Central Forecast Center in Chanhassen, Minn.

Hannah proved to be the final, fatal blow. The winter's final blizzard not only dropped an average

ANYBODY HOME?

Staff Sgt. Emil Kirschenmann of the North Dakota National Guard peers into a window of a house near the police station in Grand Forks on April 22. Two elderly women were reportedly still living there following a mandatory evacuation order.

JOSH MELTZER

APRIL

declares North Dakota a disaster area.

7 — Water from the Wild Rice and Marsh rivers forces 1,000 of Ada's 1,700 residents to evacuate.

8 — Gov. Ed Schafer activates the National Guard to help with flood-fighting efforts and blizzard recovery.

10 — East Grand Forks Flood Director Gary Sanders issues a call for 1,000 sandbaggers.

10 — FEMA Director James Lee Witt tours Ada, where floodwaters rushed in, then froze.

11 — The NWS predicts the Red River will crest during the week of April 20-27.

11 — Vice President Al Gore visits Fargo and Breckenridge, offering words of hope.

11 — Dike-walking begins in East Grand Forks.

14 — Red rises to 44.43 feet in Grand Forks.

14 — The NWS raises its crest prediction to 50 feet.

14 — Red in Fargo reaches 37.4 feet, surpassing the previous record of 37.3 feet in 1969.

15 — The Point Bridge closes in East Grand Forks.

15 — East Grand Forks Mayor Lynn Stauss says 300 to 400 Sherlock Park and Griggs Park residents may have to evacuate by nightfall. The city issues guidelines for evacuation.

15 — Due to ice jams and overland flooding, Warren suffers its third flood in less than a year.

16 — The Flood of 1997 officially becomes the Flood of the Century as the river rises above 1979's 48.88 feet.

16 — The NWS changes crest prediction to 50.5 feet.

16 — Grand Forks officials warn residents of possible evacuations.

of three inches of precipitation across the Red River basin, not only brought flood-fighting efforts to a three-day standstill and not only made dike-building more difficult and less efficient because the ground was frozen. It also brought runoff to a halt.

The blizzard and the following week of unseasonable cold caused the water to pond and pool before it all came at once with a sudden warmup. There was no normal lag time and crest movement.

"It was a screwy melt pattern," Braatz said.

That was no excuse for missing so badly, said Gary Sanders, the East Grand Forks city engineer who remains bitter over his drowned city.

He cites the water flow of 1979, when the crest reached its previous high this century of 48.8 feet. A 49-foot prediction would mean a peak flow similar to the 82,000 cubic feet per second at the height of 1979. Yet the peak flow in 1997 was 137,000 cfs.

"Missing by five feet doesn't sound like much," Sanders said. "But when you talk about flow, the National Weather Service missed by almost 100 percent."

Whether freakish nature or the NWS was most to blame, the gap between forecast and reality was an issue that never went away in the minds of those who contributed to the river of tears.

A popular sign on the mountains of debris that appeared later was: "49 feet, my ass."

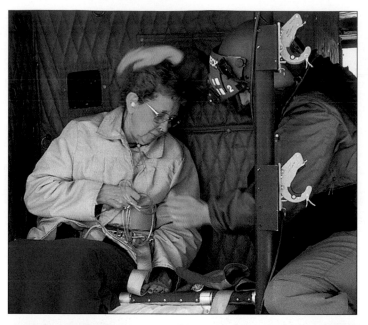

FACE OF A FIGHTER (RIGHT)
Grand Forks Mayor Pat Owens shows the strain of trying to manage her city. Owens was nicknamed "the little spitfire" for her resilience during the crisis.
JOHN DOMAN

FROM HOSPITAL TO HUEY
Grand Forks Air Force Base personnel airlift La Neva Narum, 75, from United Hospital to a Fargo hospital. All United Hospital, rehabilitation center and Valley Memorial Homes-Eldercare patients were evacuated by April 20.
JACKIE LORENTZ

DOWN, BUT NOT OUT
Weary UND student Marty Anderson rests atop a dike along Lincoln Drive. Thousands of volunteers worked around the clock fortifying dikes and filling sandbags.
JOHN STENNES

LAST MOMENTS AT HOME
Martha Hoghaug reacts on April 18 to the realization that she would lose her house on Olson Drive in Grand Forks. Hours later a dike gave way, flooding her neighborhood.
JOHN STENNES

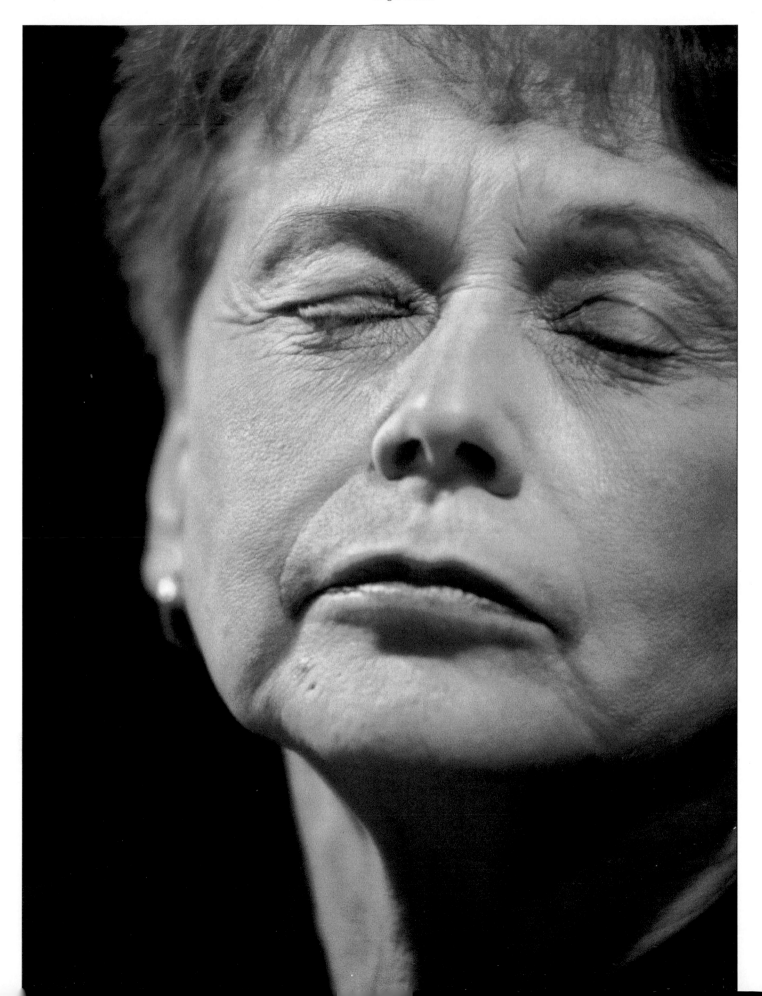

A NEIGHBORHOOD LOST FOREVER

The top of Mike Rudow's home on Lincoln Drive was about level with the Lincoln Park dike. That meant, at crest, not even his rooftop showed.

With the foot of the dike outside his back door, the 39-year-old grocery store employee knew what could happen. But he loved his small home. "It was so comfortable, for me and for everyone to visit." And he loved the location. "It was like living in town and out of town at the same time. If you wanted to get out of town, you just climbed up the dike."

Rudow was one of the last people to walk that dike. He was on dike patrol, cradling his video camera, when the sirens sounded at 4 a.m. April 18, a warning of the floodwaters that would hit four hours later.

He describes that final walk as eerie and dreary. With the power turned off, the only light came from flashlights. The sandbags stood only one foot above the river level. Dirty water bubbled through the dike, a sign that the seepage was taking the dike with it. In one place, water shot out of a hole as if from a spigot.

Rudow left the neighborhood, as the sirens ordered. But he returned later that day, helping friends retrieve belongings and watching the slow, gut-wrenching rise of the water up the walls of the homes.

After the waters receded, he stayed away for a while. "It was like I felt guilty for leaving it, like I hadn't done enough. I loved my home."

But he did go back, only to find his refrigera-

MAKING WAVES

Jason Schmidt of the North Dakota National Guard watches his wake as he drives a five-ton truck on 15th Avenue South in Grand Forks on April 24. More than 300 National Guardsmen were deployed throughout Greater Grand Forks.

ERIC HYLDEN

KNEE-DEEP DESPITE ORDERS

Chris Sveningson wades along Belmont Road at 47th Avenue South to check his house on April 22 even though the area was declared a mandatory evacuation area. Nearly three-fourths of Grand Forks was under a mandatory evacuation order because of floodwaters and unsafe living conditions.

JOSH MELTZER

tor wedged on the hallway steps, preventing him from going into the basement. "It was like someone was telling me not to go down there."

In June, he went back more often, each time finding something else worth salvaging. He was there when a construction worker told him of the impending demolition of his neighborhood. The emptiness grew inside him.

"One day I have a home and the next day I don't. I didn't do anything to hurt anyone. It was just an act of nature. You'd see other disasters and not know how those people felt. When it hits home, you know."

FLOODING HAD DOMINO EFFECT

The beginning of the end for Grand Forks came in the Lincoln Drive neighborhood. From there, the water had a domino effect, running north and west down streets and storm sewers.

At the corner of Belmont Road and 13th Avenue South, a makeshift dike broke at about 8 a.m. Knee-deep water spilled down streets and cascaded along Lincoln Drive, which became a foaming spillway. Once that filled, the water continued to seek its own level.

"Once the water got inside the dikes and into the storm sewers, there was no stopping it," city engineer Ken Vein said. "The land is lower to the north, so it headed that way. And even a full mile west of the river, it's almost the same elevation."

The city tried to stop the flow early with impromptu dikes down

A CANINE GREETING

Blue, a Great Dane belonging to the owners of Valley Queen Laundromat, stands in the doorway to greet customers. Laundromats in Grand Forks and East Grand Forks felt a rush of business from flood-stricken residents who lost their washers and dryers.

ELIZABETH HEFELFINGER

alleys and streets, but both material and equipment ran out. The flood fight was designed to handle 51 to 52 feet, Vein said, not 54.

So the water moved north, down Belmont Road and Reeves Drive. It reached the Central Park area in early evening, then flowed toward downtown. A defining moment came when the Emergency Operations Center located in the

police building had to head for higher ground. It was about 9:30 p.m.

It was about that point that the focus changed. Mayor Pat Owens urged the entire city to evacuate.

"We were no longer fighting the flood; we had changed the emphasis to saving lives," Vein said. "Seeing the water spread was devastating. I didn't want to give up, but I knew for the protection

APRIL

16 — Walsh County officials urge the evacuation of homes and farmsteads east of I-29 and west of the Red River north of Grand Forks.

17 — Red stands at 50.96 feet. NWS raises prediction again to 51.5 feet.

17 — About 1 p.m., hundreds of Lincoln Drive residents evacuate after reports that a nearby dike had broken. The dike is repaired.

17 — East Grand Forks Mayor Lynn Stauss' battle cry of "two feet in two days" urges residents to raise dikes to meet rising crest predictions.

17 — Red River breaks through a clay dike south of Bygland, filling a coulee that passes through East Grand Forks.

April 18 — 20
An hourly chronology
is on Page 38.

21 — Red River crests at 54.11 feet.

21 — Demolition of burnt-out buildings begins.

21 — Classes are canceled for the rest of the year in Grand Forks and East Grand Forks schools.

21 — Emergency Animal Rescue Service sets out in search of pets left behind.

22 — President Clinton tours devastated area via helicopter.
22 — At least 1,500 Pembina and Drayton residents leave homes as dikes crack.
22 — Mayville (N.D.) State University cancels classes.

of life that we had to do it. Today looking back, that's what I'm most proud of."

Vein said he held some hope that the railroad tracks running through downtown would serve as a barrier, stopping the water as it flowed north. But the water topped the tracks, and as the streets filled up, and then the sewers, the water moved to the next block. By Saturday morning, downtown was flooded and the overtaking of the Riverside Park area had begun.

By Saturday afternoon, the water had traveled a mile from the river, several blocks west of Washington Street, where residents were stunned by its presence and by how fast it came. By Sunday, 80 percent of the city was covered by chocolate-colored water.

STUBBORN FIGHT TO A BITTER END

Every day that week, Myrna Flint woke up vowing to move family belongings out of their home in the Griggs Park neighborhood in East Grand Forks. And every day, the magnetic pull of the dike proved too strong.

"I can't be here; I have to get up there and help sandbag," she'd tell herself. "I want to save the house. I want to save the neighborhood."

So she'd throw sandbags for 12 to 14 hours, and the fatigue she felt at day's end left no muscle power nor emotional power to clear a house that had been home for 19 years.

Even on April 18, when big trouble was brewing, Myrna joined her husband, Jerry, atop the levee, flood-fighting still

A CRUISE THROUGH CHAOS

Elizabeth Dole, left, president of the American Red Cross, talks with Nancy Jones Schafer, first lady of North Dakota, and Grand Forks Mayor Pat Owens while touring the flooded downtown area of Grand Forks on April 23. The Red Cross was one of several relief organizations helping citizens of Greater Grand Forks recover from the flood disaster.

JACKIE LORENTZ

"Water cannot wash that away, fire cannot burn that away, and a blizzard cannot freeze that away."

BILL CLINTON, president of the United States, talking about the valley's spirit and faith

taking priority over possession-saving.

"Besides, we thought, worst-case scenario would have a foot or so on the main floor and we'd have to cut the Sheetrock up four feet," Myrna said.

That fateful Friday night, Myrna and Jerry were on the dike again. But the pumps below were no longer keeping pace with the seepage. Jerry urged her to leave. No way, she said. Too much investment to retreat now.

A few minutes later, Myrna lost track of Jerry, who was walking the dike with a walkie-talkie. She feared the worst. "I got real scared. When I found him again and he told me again to leave, I told him that not only wasn't I leaving, but he wasn't leaving my sight."

Shortly before midnight, Army Corps of Engineers workers roared into the neighborhood to declare the battle lost. Get out now, they said. The water had topped the dike several blocks away at the north end of the

THE PRESIDENT SPEAKS

President Clinton speaks at Grand Forks Air Force Base on April 22 just days after massive flooding turned the city into a disaster area. The president promised $500 million in flood relief.

ERIC HYLDEN

APRIL

23 — UND President Kendall Baker offers facilities to residents and businesses.

23 — Red River begins to recede.

23 — American Red Cross President Elizabeth Dole tours flood-stricken area with North Dakota first lady Nancy Jones Schafer and Grand Forks Mayor Pat Owens.

24 — Some Grand Forks residents are allowed to visit their homes for a few hours.

24 — Volunteers work to save Pembina from floodwaters.

25 — House Speaker Newt Gingrich visits the region.

26 — Property damage estimated at $775 million in Grand Forks and East Grand Forks.

26 — The first portion of East Grand Forks reopens to residents. Portions of Grand Forks continue to open.

27 — A Northwest Airlines 747 arrives in Grand Forks with 200,000 pounds of flood-relief goods.

27 — Interstate 29 reopens between Grand Forks and Fargo, eliminating a one-hour detour through Casselton, N.D.

28 — The Kennedy Bridge reopens after 10 days, uniting Grand Forks and East Grand Forks.

28 — The Grand Forks City Council meets for the first time since the disaster.

29 — An anonymous woman, "Angel," pledges to give $2,000 to every household hurt by floodwaters.

A MAYOR'S NIGHTMARE
A Coast Guard boat carrying East Grand Forks Mayor Lynn Stauss passes in front of flooded houses during a tour of River Road in East Grand Forks on April 24.

CHUCK KIMMERLE

Louis Murray Memorial Bridge and was headed toward Griggs Park. The dike that the neighborhood had worked to fortify on the Red was now being attacked from the rear, outflanked by the Red Lake River. Water poured into the neighborhood from the hill behind the Consource convenience store, and it gushed from manholes like fountains.

Myrna remembered the emergency stash in her kitchen — a slow cooker, some clothes in a laundry basket, utensils — little stuff. She knew it was too late for the living room and bedroom furniture, the appliances and everything else a family of four accumulates over 19 years. But the little stuff, the barest of necessities, tugged at her. Jerry

"I never thought I'd be taking a boat ride down DeMers Avenue."

EARL POMEROY,
U.S. congressman

GETTING A DOG OUT OF WATER
Animal rescue volunteers Scott Frederick, front, and Brad Merchant, back, bring in a rescued Chesapeake Bay retriever on April 23. The dog had been trapped in a garage with two feet of river water for five days. More than 700 animals were rescued from flooded homes in Grand Forks and East Grand Forks.

JOHN DOMAN

tugged back, and they headed to higher ground.

"It was scary because the water came in fast," Myrna said. "The water running down the street wasn't over my boots, but it was close. I just hung on to Jerry, and we walked."

They then went to tell daughters Jenny, 14, and Mistie, 12, the news. The tears began. More tears came in the afternoon when the family stood on the railroad tracks and saw water up to the eaves of their home. Photo albums, put on the second floor "to be safe for sure," were ruined.

Jerry grew up in the house, which his parents built in 1948. "I'm sure it's harder on Jerry, but he's not talking about it," Myrna said.

The Flints won't return to live in that house. It's been condemned. They're living in an apartment this summer — but

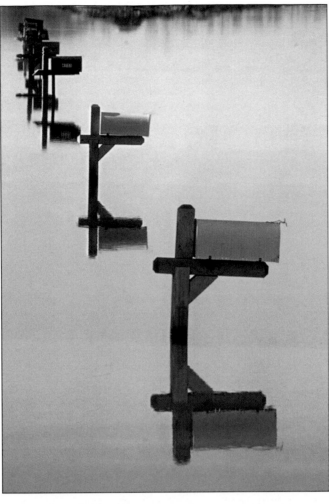

"The Red River is bringing us together to build our community. It's not something that separates us; it's something that brings us together."

LYNN STAUSS,
East Grand Forks mayor

REFLECTIONS IN THE RED

Mailboxes sit in three feet of water on Belmont Road during the crest.

JOSH MELTZER

SEARCH AND RESCUE

Members of the U.S. Coast Guard patrol the Lincoln Drive area of Grand Forks on April 19. By 2 p.m. that day, all of Grand Forks east of Columbia Road was under a mandatory evacuation order.

JOHN STENNES

Three tragic days

FRIDAY, APRIL 18

2:45 a.m. — Red River at 51.42.

4:15 a.m. — Boils appear in the Lincoln Park dike. City orders evacuation, including 106 residents of Valley Memorial Homes-Almonte Living Center.

6 a.m. — City orders evacuation of Riverside and Central Park areas.

8 a.m. — Water runs out of north end of Lincoln Park Golf Course and down Lincoln Drive.

11:15 a.m. — "It's one of the major disasters of our lifetime," Grand Forks Mayor Pat Owens tells CNN television.

11:35 a.m. — National Weather Service revises its crest projection to 53 for today or Saturday.

Noon — River at 52.19.

12:15 p.m. — First break in East Grand Forks dikes comes near Folson Park. But ring dike temporarily saves area.

3:30 p.m. — Dike just south of Murray Bridge in East Grand Forks breaks, resulting in the flooding of entire Point area.

4 p.m. — Sirens sound as Point area ordered evacuated, and Murray Bridge closes.

4:30 p.m. — Water in Lincoln Drive area reaches same level as river, leaving about 300 homes in water, many of them to the rooftops.

7:14 p.m. — River reaches 52.62, up 18 inches in 18 hours.

8:08 p.m. — NWS revises crest for 54.0 feet on Saturday.

8:20 p.m. — Central Park area fills rapidly.

9:40 p.m. — Emergency Operations Center at Grand Forks police station moves to UND as storm sewer backup runs down Fifth Street. Within 30 minutes, the police station basement is full of water.

10 p.m. — River reaches 52.76; Owens bans sale of alcohol in Grand Forks.

11 p.m. — EGF dike near Kennedy Bridge fails, cutting the last link between the two cities and flooding Sherlock Park homes.

SATURDAY, APRIL 19

Midnight — Water flows off dike by Murray Bridge, flooding land inside Griggs Park in EGF.

1 a.m. — Water comes over the dike by Valley Golf Course in EGF.

2:20 a.m. — Herald pressroom and mailroom employees flee building as sewer backup water rushes down the alley and threatens to overtake downtown.

4 a.m. — With two feet of water in the lobby, senior citizens are carried from Ryan House.

4 a.m. — Dikes are topped and downtown East Grand Forks — the city's last dry area — is flooded.

5 a.m. — Water is four feet deep in downtown Grand Forks.

6 a.m. — River at 52.89.

7:10 a.m. — Water tops the dike in Riverside Park.

7:50 a.m. — National Guard begins diking EGF Police Department.

8 a.m. — Grand Forks water plant fails.

10 a.m. — City orders evacuation of all areas in Grand Forks east of Washington Street.

11 a.m. — UND President Kendall Baker calls off classes for the semester, two weeks before final exams are to start.

Noon — Approximately 50 percent of Grand Forks and virtually all of East Grand Forks are flooded.

1 p.m. — Riverside Park area is filled with floodwater.

2 p.m. — Area east of Columbia Road ordered evacuated.

4:15 p.m. — Fire reported in Security Building, 101 N. Third St.

7 p.m. — Ninety percent of EGF's 8,700 residents have been evacuated.

7:15 p.m. — Planes begin dropping chemical retardant on fire.

8 p.m. — Fire has spread to three city blocks.

10 p.m. — Approximately 4,000 EGF evacuees have arrived in Crookston.

SUNDAY, APRIL 20

5:30 a.m. — Eleven buildings are either lost or heavily damaged by the fire.

7 a.m. — River at 53.7.

10 a.m. — Grand Forks water supply exhausted.

11:30 a.m. — Owens announces 24-hour curfew in mandatory evacuation zones.

2 p.m. — A helicopter dumps water on the smoldering downtown fire.

7 p.m. — United Hospital evacuates the last of its patients.

8 p.m. — 75 percent of Grand Forks' residents are evacuated.

9 p.m. — River at 53.99.

> "*I'm the first mayor to lose a town; that's how devastating it is.*"
>
> **Lynn Stauss,**
> East Grand Forks mayor
> April 19, 1997

SHIELDING FROM THE SPLASH

John Fick turns his head from the spray of a sump pump that's draining the area behind the dike at his Lake Drive home on April 18.

CHUCK KIMMERLE

FIRST LOOKS AT LINCOLN

Michelle Hovet looks in horror at the flooded homes in the Lincoln Park area on April 18. By early evening, water had reached the roofs of the houses.

BILL ALKOFER

MAY

1 — FEMA announces it will bring 100 fully equipped trailers for evacuees.

2 — Nondrinkable water is restored in Grand Forks.

2 — United Hospital reopens its emergency room.

2 — The Red River crests at Winnipeg, leaving the town virtually unscathed.

3 — UND students return to campus to clear out their dorm rooms.

3 — Experts say this wasn't a 500-year flood, but the next flood could be worse, and it could come soon.

4 — North Dakota's Congressional delegation requests an explanation from the National Weather Service and the Army Corps of Engineers on why they didn't share information that might have offered a more accurate flood forecast.

4 — State fire investigators begin probing the cause of the downtown fire that destroyed 11 buildings.

5 — Mayor Owens issues order banning scavengers from picking through debris on the berms.

8 — A second "angel" gives $5 million for the people of Greater Grand Forks.

9 — East Grand Forks gets potable water for the first time in three weeks.

9 — Army Corps of Engineers releases a map pushing the proposed dike line farther back than one drawn by city engineers.

11 — The Point Bridge reopens.

12 — Drinkable tap water is restored to Grand Forks.

14 — FEMA Director James Lee Witt tours area to assess flood damage.

15 — Mayor Owens meets with first lady Hillary Clinton in Washington, D.C.

18 — The Herald reports that McDonald's heiress Joan Kroc is the "Angel" who donated $2,000 to each head of household in Greater Grand Forks.

A river takes two cities

Grand Forks and East Grand Forks prepared for the worst. Based on a predicted crest by the National Weather Service of 49 feet, dikes are built to protect both cities to 52 feet. The river eventually crests at 54.11 feet, and weary officials, unable to keep ahead of the rapidly rising water, let nature take its course.

April 16 Wednesday

Worried officials ask residents of the Riverside Park, Central Park and Lincoln Drive areas to evacuate their homes. There is concern the dikes in those areas are not safe and may give way.

April 17 Thursday

River reaches 50 feet, 22 feet above flood stage. Lincoln Drive area is evacuated about 1 p.m. when transfer cracks in dike are discovered. Some residents return home later after cracks are repaired. Sandbagging efforts continue in both cities.

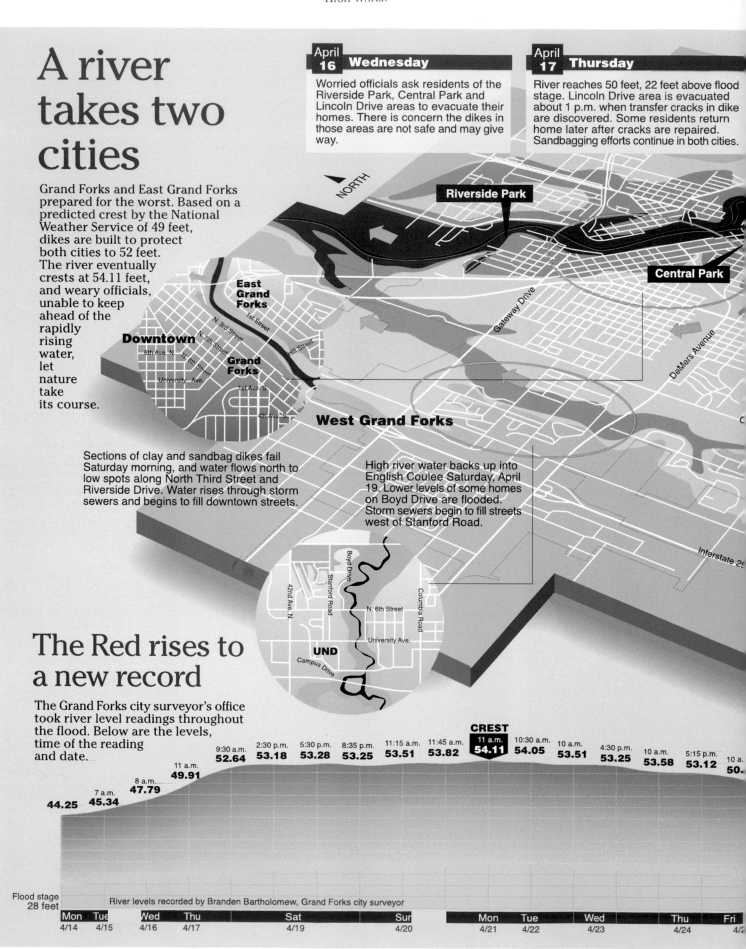

NORTH

Riverside Park

Central Park

East Grand Forks

Downtown

Grand Forks

Gateway Drive

DeMers Avenue

West Grand Forks

Interstate 29

N. 3rd Street
N. 5th Street
N. 8th Street
6th Ave. N.
University Ave.
1st Ave. S.
4th Ave. S.
1st Street
Hill Street

Sections of clay and sandbag dikes fail Saturday morning, and water flows north to low spots along North Third Street and Riverside Drive. Water rises through storm sewers and begins to fill downtown streets.

High river water backs up into English Coulee Saturday, April 19. Lower levels of some homes on Boyd Drive are flooded. Storm sewers begin to fill streets west of Stanford Road.

Boyd Drive
Stanford Road
42nd Ave. N.
N. 6th Street
Columbia Road
University Ave.
UND
Campus Drive

The Red rises to a new record

The Grand Forks city surveyor's office took river level readings throughout the flood. Below are the levels, time of the reading and date.

Time	Level
7 a.m.	44.25
	45.34
8 a.m.	47.79
11 a.m.	49.91
9:30 a.m.	52.64
2:30 p.m.	53.18
5:30 p.m.	53.28
8:35 p.m.	53.25
11:15 a.m.	53.51
11:45 a.m.	53.82
CREST 11 a.m.	54.11
10:30 a.m.	54.05
10 a.m.	53.51
4:30 p.m.	53.25
10 a.m.	53.58
5:15 p.m.	53.12
10 a.	50.

Flood stage 28 feet

River levels recorded by Branden Bartholomew, Grand Forks city surveyor

Mon 4/14	Tue 4/15	Wed 4/16	Thu 4/17	Sat 4/19	Sun 4/20	Mon 4/21	Tue 4/22	Wed 4/23	Thu 4/24	Fri 4/2

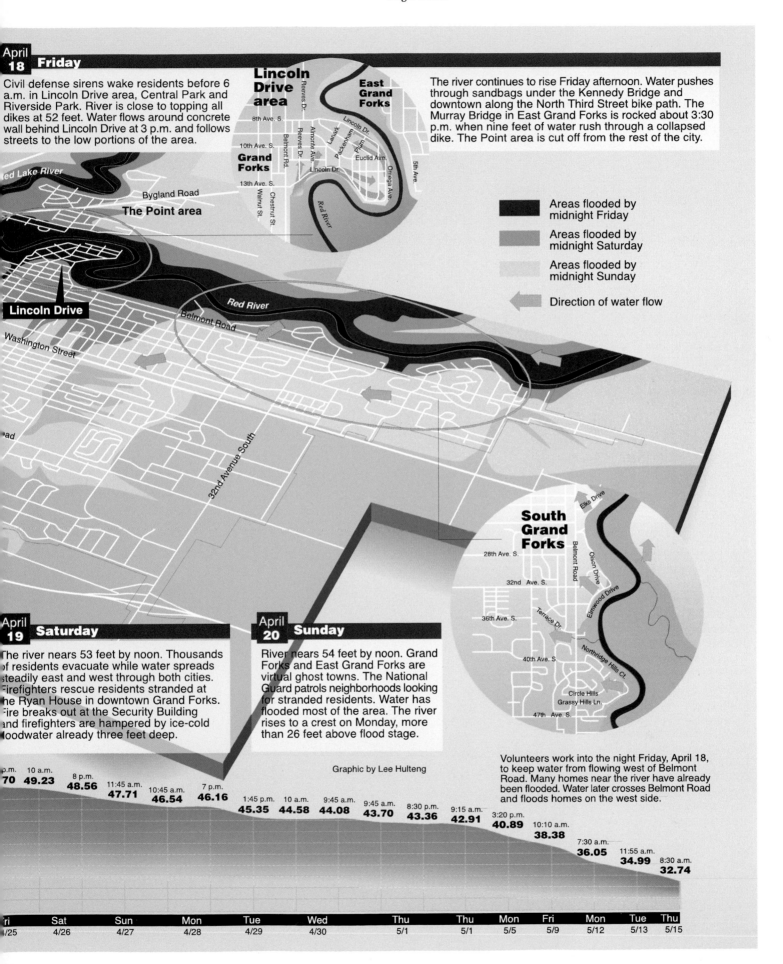

April 18 Friday

Civil defense sirens wake residents before 6 a.m. in Lincoln Drive area, Central Park and Riverside Park. River is close to topping all dikes at 52 feet. Water flows around concrete wall behind Lincoln Drive at 3 p.m. and follows streets to the low portions of the area.

The river continues to rise Friday afternoon. Water pushes through sandbags under the Kennedy Bridge and downtown along the North Third Street bike path. The Murray Bridge in East Grand Forks is rocked about 3:30 p.m. when nine feet of water rush through a collapsed dike. The Point area is cut off from the rest of the city.

Lincoln Drive area

8th Ave. S.
10th Ave. S.
13th Ave. S.
Grand Forks
Reeves Dr.
Belmont Rd.
Reeves Dr.
Almonte Ave.
Lanark
Packenham
Lincoln Dr.
Lincoln Dr.
Euclid Ave.
Onega Ave.
5th Ave.
Walnut St.
Chestnut St.

East Grand Forks

Ed Lake River

Bygland Road

The Point area

Lincoln Drive

Washington Street

Red River

Belmont Road

32nd Avenue South

- Areas flooded by midnight Friday
- Areas flooded by midnight Saturday
- Areas flooded by midnight Sunday
- Direction of water flow

South Grand Forks

28th Ave. S.
32nd Ave. S.
36th Ave. S.
40th Ave. S.
47th Ave. S.
Elks Drive
Belmont Road
Olson Drive
Elmwood Drive
Terrace Dr.
Northridge Hills Ct.
Circle Hills
Grassy Hills Ln.

April 19 Saturday

The river nears 53 feet by noon. Thousands of residents evacuate while water spreads steadily east and west through both cities. Firefighters rescue residents stranded at the Ryan House in downtown Grand Forks. Fire breaks out at the Security Building and firefighters are hampered by ice-cold floodwater already three feet deep.

April 20 Sunday

River nears 54 feet by noon. Grand Forks and East Grand Forks are virtual ghost towns. The National Guard patrols neighborhoods looking for stranded residents. Water has flooded most of the area. The river rises to a crest on Monday, more than 26 feet above flood stage.

Graphic by Lee Hulteng

Volunteers work into the night Friday, April 18, to keep water from flowing west of Belmont Road. Many homes near the river have already been flooded. Water later crosses Belmont Road and floods homes on the west side.

p.m.	10 a.m.	8 p.m.	11:45 a.m.	10:45 a.m.	7 p.m.	1:45 p.m.	10 a.m.	9:45 a.m.	9:45 a.m.	8:30 p.m.	9:15 a.m.	3:20 p.m.	10:10 a.m.	7:30 a.m.	11:55 a.m.	8:30 a.m.
70	49.23	48.56	47.71	46.54	46.16	45.35	44.58	44.08	43.70	43.36	42.91	40.89	38.38	36.05	34.99	32.74

ri	Sat	Sun	Mon	Tue	Wed	Thu	Thu	Mon	Fri	Mon	Tue	Thu
/25	4/26	4/27	4/28	4/29	4/30	5/1	5/1	5/5	5/9	5/12	5/13	5/15

almost every night they return to Griggs Park to talk to the people who made it a neighborhood.

"The apartment is not home. But East Grand Forks is," Myrna said.

So, plans are to move to a property just outside the city limits. "It's away from the river," Myrna said.

EGF's POINT
FLOODED FIRST

In East Grand Forks, the Point went first. A few blocks southeast of the Murray Bridge, a dike holding back the Red Lake River collapsed about 3:30 p.m. on April 18. Nine feet of water surged into the neighborhood. The force of it rocked the bridge. The break cut the Point off from the rest of the city and slowly began flooding the neighborhood.

When backup from the Hartsville Coulee cut off escape to the south later in the day, Point residents had to be evacuated by helicopter.

"With the Hartsville carrying backup flow from the Red, we actually had three rivers attack us this time," said Sanders, the city engineer.

East Grand Forks not only lost a portion of town when the Point succumbed, it also lost a big share of its diking work force. Flood-fighters had to tend to families and homes.

Sherlock Park went next, when a dike on the north side of the Kennedy Bridge failed about 11 p.m. Water flowed under the U.S. Highway 2 underpass and poured into Sherlock Park as sandbaggers fled.

Continued on page 49

ALONE IN AN ABYSS

A commuter bus lies on its side April 24 after being toppled by the Red River floodwaters in Grand Forks.

SCOTT TAKUSHI

Red River
Crests

KEY

Winnipeg
18 | 24.5 | May 3
Flood stage ┘ └ 1997 crest └ Date of crest

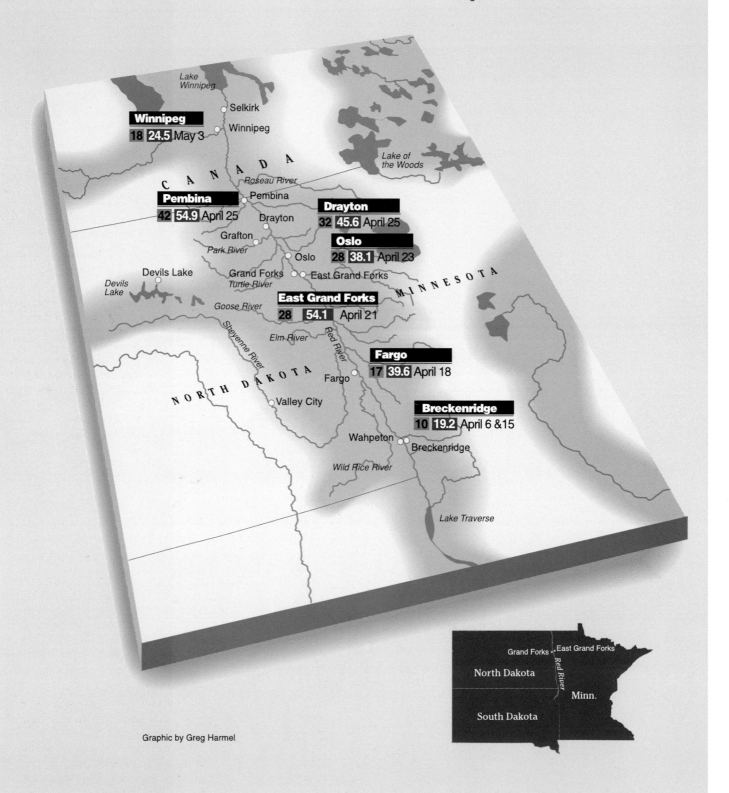

Lake Winnipeg

Selkirk

Winnipeg

Winnipeg
18 | 24.5 | May 3

Lake of the Woods

C A N A D A

Roseau River

Pembina

Pembina
42 | 54.9 | April 25

Drayton

Drayton
32 | 45.6 | April 25

Grafton

Park River

Oslo

Oslo
28 | 38.1 | April 23

Devils Lake

Devils Lake

Grand Forks

Turtle River

East Grand Forks

M I N N E S O T A

Goose River

East Grand Forks
28 | 54.1 | April 21

Sheyenne River

Elm River

Red River

Fargo
17 | 39.6 | April 18

N O R T H   D A K O T A

Fargo

Valley City

Breckenridge
10 | 19.2 | April 6 & 15

Wahpeton

Breckenridge

Wild Rice River

Lake Traverse

Graphic by Greg Harmel

Grand Forks · East Grand Forks

North Dakota

Red River

Minn.

South Dakota

44

22 — Congress recesses for Memorial Day without finishing work on a disaster relief bill.

24 — A National Weather Service team arrives in North Dakota to investigate the flood forecasts.

29 — American Red Cross begins to pull out of Grand Forks.

JUNE

9 — The U.S. Army Corps of Engineers proposes three flood-protection plans for Greater Grand Forks.

9 — President Clinton vetoes disaster-aid bill because it contains provisions not related to disasters.

12 — President Clinton signs revised $8.6 billion disaster-aid bill.

WATER EVERYWHERE

Tombstones at Memorial Park Cemetery sit underwater on April 24. Some graves collapsed, and only one Grand Forks cemetery was fit for Memorial Day services a month later.

ERIC HYLDEN

THE RED'S NEW TOYS
A stuffed animal floats in the floodwaters of the Red River near the Kennedy Bridge in East Grand Forks on April 26.

JOHN STENNES

A MUD DUCK
A rubber duck sits encrusted in dried Red River mud.

CANDACE BARBOT

STORE WITH A VIEW
From the window of Dakota TV and Appliance in downtown Grand Forks on April 21, a poster of the Maytag repairman surveys the floodwaters running down North Fourth Street.

JOSH MELTZER

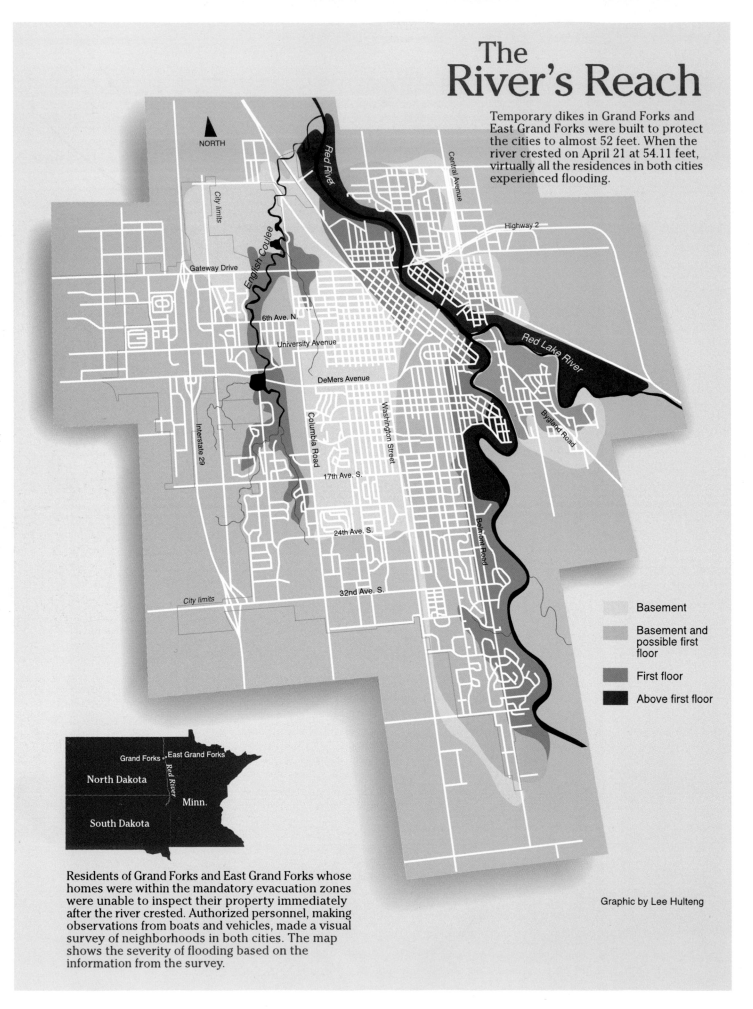

The River's Reach

Temporary dikes in Grand Forks and East Grand Forks were built to protect the cities to almost 52 feet. When the river crested on April 21 at 54.11 feet, virtually all the residences in both cities experienced flooding.

NORTH

Red River

City limits

English Coulee

Gateway Drive

6th Ave. N.

University Avenue

DeMers Avenue

Interstate 29

Columbia Road

Washington Street

17th Ave. S.

24th Ave. S.

City limits

32nd Ave. S.

Central Avenue

Highway 2

Red Lake River

Bygland Road

Belmont Road

Basement

Basement and possible first floor

First floor

Above first floor

Grand Forks · East Grand Forks

North Dakota

Red River

Minn.

South Dakota

Residents of Grand Forks and East Grand Forks whose homes were within the mandatory evacuation zones were unable to inspect their property immediately after the river crested. Authorized personnel, making observations from boats and vehicles, made a visual survey of neighborhoods in both cities. The map shows the severity of flooding based on the information from the survey.

Graphic by Lee Hulteng

A Northern Reflection
The Northern Lights are reflected in floodwaters lining Interstate 29 near Manvel, N.D.

Continued from page 42

As Friday turned into Saturday, the dike near the Valley Golf Course was overpowered, and the Griggs Park neighborhood was flooded from the back door when the north side of the Murray Bridge was overtaken. Downtown went last, about 4 a.m.

"We couldn't put any more dirt on top, and no volunteers were left to sandbag," Sanders said about downtown.

For the 10 miles of dikes in East Grand Forks, 52.6 feet was the breaking point. And with the entire city lost to the rivers, Sanders reached his breaking point. He left with his family for his lake cabin Saturday afternoon.

"Enough was enough," he explained. "And we weren't fighting the flood anymore."

Prayer for Evacuees
Dear Lord, we thank you that you are our refuge and our strength.

Father, we pray for all who are leaving and have left our city. Send an angel to watch over us and to keep us as we live these next weeks in new homes. Thanks for the many who are lovingly providing for us.

Dear Lord, be with all our people, and as the waters subside, lead us safely home again. Amen.

Rev. Norm Beighley,
Trinity Lutheran Church,
Manvel, N.D.

When it couldn't get any worse...

A DARK DOWNTOWN
Black smoke pours out of downtown Grand Forks the evening of April 19, a few hours after the blaze started in the Security Building.

JOHN DOMAN

From snow to ice to flood. It couldn't get any worse. Could it?

It could. Fire. About 4 p.m. April 19, a fire broke out in the Security Building in downtown Grand Forks that eventually spread to 11 buildings.

Not only was the heart of the city in flames, but the hearts of its people were, too. Where would it all end, they wondered? Jerry Anderson, the battalion chief whose crew was first on the scene, shared those feelings.

"Even though everything was terrible because of the flood, you at least believed that the worst that could possibly happen had already happened," Anderson said. "It hadn't.

"That really sets you back."

And the fight was set back at least an hour because firefighters first had to evacuate about 40 apartment-dwellers on the block who had defied repeated evacuation orders.

"We had to take care of the people first," Anderson said. "People are No. 1. Firefighting has to take second place."

A BATTLE FOR THE CITY
Grand Forks firefighters Mike Sande, left, and Randy Johnson battle the April 19 fire that destroyed 11 downtown buildings. Firefighters evacuated about 40 apartment-dwellers before they could begin fighting the fire.

BILL ALKOFER

A RED CLOUD OF HOPE
    A fire-bombing plane, usually used in forest fires, drops fire retardant on the downtown blaze. The fire was reported at 4:15 p.m. April 19 and was still being fought 22 hours later.

CHUCK KIMMERLE

"They've trained for some wild scenarios, but nothing like this."

CAPT. DUANE LUND,
Grand Forks
Fire Department

BOMBS AWAY

An air crane helicopter dumps a bucket of water on smoldering downtown flames. Helicopters made 60 drops of 2,000 gallons of water on the fire, a total of 120,000 gallons.

JOHN STENNES

Meanwhile, the fire burned wider and hotter. Then came more frustrations, the greatest of them being the cruel irony of the four feet of water on the streets that prevented water from being cast on the flames.

Most of the trucks couldn't get through the high water on the streets. A pumper made it but then worked for only two minutes before the truck's motor blew from taking on eight gallons of water, spewing an oily slick. Then there was no water pressure in the fire hydrants.

"Everything we do in fighting fires is dependent on your equipment and your water supply, and

we couldn't use either," Anderson said.

Fire retardant dropped from an airplane was used before fire trucks finally reached the area atop flat-bed trucks. Sixty drops of 2,000 gallons each from a helicopter bucket finished the job the next day.

By then, some buildings were charred shells, roofless and windowless. The fire had wiped out the west side of North Third Street from the Security Building to the Grand Forks Herald and had hopscotched over other buildings to two other blocks.

The fire was caused by an electrical problem triggered by the floodwater.

A FUTILE FIGHT

Grand Forks firefighters douse a hot spot at the Security Building on April 25, six days after the fire began. The fire truck was placed on a National Guard flat-bed truck because it couldn't operate in the high water.

RICHARD WISDOM

"Everything we do in fighting fires is dependent on your equipment and your water supply, and we couldn't use either."

JERRY ANDERSON,
battalion chief, Grand Forks Fire Department

A CITY CRUMBLES

The Security Building, home to several small businesses, stands in ruins on April 20 despite the heroic efforts of frustrated firefighters.

ERIC HYLDEN

The scene left lasting impressions on Tina Hulst and Mitch Steien, among others.

Hulst had stayed at her home on University Avenue, feeling safe despite the water.

"What scared us out is the fire," she said. "It kept going. All we saw was the fire shooting up. Sparks were flying everywhere."

Steien, a firefighter, described his ordeal as "unreal, beyond my wildest imagination." Even though he's 6-foot-6 and 270 pounds, he said he needed all his might to stand in the current. And he needed all his alertness to dodge ice chunks and file cabinets that traveled with the swift current.

After standing in 38-degree water in hip-waders for about an hour, Steien was one of three firefighters hospitalized for hypothermia.

"I've always only wished we could have done more," he said.

Grand Forks lessons help northern neighbors

Communities to the north looked at Breckenridge, Ada, Grand Forks and East Grand Forks and feared the worst.

For most, the fear was greater than the reality.

The hamlet of Robbin, Minn., had no defenses and was submerged, but no other town along the Red River had to bear the same misery as the scarred cities to the south.

Luck and effort were the twin reasons for their survival.

In Warren, Minn., residents were ready for the third flood from the Snake River in less than a year. Even though about two-thirds of the homes had seepage and the eastern half of town had water for seven days, sandbags and pumps minimized the damage because of early preparations.

In Crookston, a neighborhood came a few inches and a few minutes from flooding when an ice jam backed up the water. But heavy equipment got the ice flowing, and the Red Lake River quickly dropped two feet.

"We were a blink of an

A Scene at the Frontlines

A grain elevator in Drayton, N.D., reflects on the flooded Red River at sunrise. In the foreground, a plywood-and-sandbag-reinforced dike protects the town from floodwaters.

J. Albert Diaz

FARMLAND FLOODED
A grain elevator
north of Drayton, N.D.,
is isolated by the
flooded Red River.
About 5.4 million acres
of farmland were
underwater in North
Dakota and Minnesota.
JOE ROSSI

eye away from being
another Ada," said Floyd
Spence, Crookston's
emergency director.

In towns such as
Mayville, Portland,
Hillsboro, Grafton, Minto
and Neche in North
Dakota and Hendrum,
Halstad and St. Vincent in
Minnesota, armies of vol-
unteers held back the
rivers flowing toward the
Red.

North of Grand Forks
on the Red, the water
level didn't come close to
the revised crest predic-
tions. Instead, the channel
bulged out, spreading the
river sideways. The Red
was as much as 25 miles
wide in some places.

Almost everyone in
Drayton left town, but
when they returned, they
found homes high and
dry, protected by dogged
diking. Drayton prepared
for a crest of 48 to 49 feet.
The river reached only
45.5 feet.

"We held off the water,"
Drayton flood coordinator
LaVern Zimmerman said.
"We had a little more time
than Grand Forks when
we knew how high it was
going to get. The water
heading eight miles over-
land certainly helped,
too."

In Pembina, 20 homes
in the unprotected south
part of town were lost.
But most of Pembina was
saved by a homemade
plywood dike. The job
was easier because the
river stopped rising three

BUILDING A WALL

(RIGHT)

Drayton resident Wesley Ladouceur, left, and Gary Gross of Milton, N.D., drive a post into the top of a dike. Residents dubbed the dike "The Great Wall of Drayton."

JOE ROSSI

(BOTTOM)

The shadow of a man pounding in a post on a dike on April 23 is cast on the wall of a Drayton building.

DAVID P. GILKEY

feet before it reached its predicted crest.

That makeshift structure, sandbags stuffed inside the plywood walls like ground pork in sausage casings, was just one reason that Pembina was the Little Town that Could.

At age 200, Pembina is North Dakota's oldest city. It is also the state's lowest-lying city and its last outpost on the Red. Pembina has a history of annual dealings with the river and its tributary, the Pembina River. Residents weren't going to surrender easily. Ordered to evacuate, they resisted.

"We have the people to put up the fight," Mayor Hetty Walker said. "We are safe. Why panic?"

Elected officials eventually agreed, allowing some workers to remain behind to complete diking. They did, and most of the town was saved for its bicentennial celebration.

Then there was Oslo, Minn. Life went on normally there — except that residents had to use boats to get in and out of the town, which remained an island in the flood. There was one problem. The permanent dikes put up by the U.S. Army Corps of Engineers in

DRENCHING A DRIFT

(TOP)

Wes Smith of St. Thomas, N.D., uses a hose hooked to a sump pump in an attempt to cut channels through a 15-foot snowdrift in his front yard on April 27. Smith was carving the snowbank to quicken the melt.

JOE ROSSI

WATER VS. WATER

(BOTTOM)

Drayton City Superintendent Ron Helm keeps a watchful eye on the river's rise outside the water plant on April 26. Helm kept the plant functioning during the flood. The building's letters dropped as the snowdrifts covering them melted.

CAROLYN KASTER

1966 needed to be watered to hold down the dust.

When the crest reached Winnipeg, it was anticlimactic. Water spread out across southern Manitoba's farmland. Ste. Agathe was engulfed. Grande Pointe fought water and lost some houses. Winnipeg prepared for a fight, erecting a dike south of the city and using some 7 million sandbags.

But a diversion ditch, the Winnipeg Floodway,

steered water around Winnipeg. Premier Duff Roblin pushed the ditch after the Flood of 1950. When he appeared in public after the Flood of 1997, grateful Winnipeggers gave him a 10-minute ovation.

Canadians seemed more worried about 100,000 dead cows that were rumored to be on their way down the Red. But, no, Americans didn't send any Holsteins. Just lots of water.

59

THE RED'S EXPANSE (PREVIOUS PAGES)
　Don Mozinski walks in the Red River floodwaters that inundated his family farm in Ardoch, N.D., on April 26. The Red River is normally six miles east of his farm.

CAROLYN KASTER

EXHAUSTED (ABOVE)
　Ashleigh Chisholm, 15, rests on top of a mound of sand while helping to fill sandbags for use in Manvel, N.D., on April 21.

JOSH MELTZER

THE NEW RIVER ROAD

A sightseer from Canada takes a look at the new channel of the Pembina River — through North Dakota Highway 18. The break in the highway was made so that the water could move faster through the area and reduce backup.

J. ALBERT DIAZ

CANADIAN INFANTRY

Twenty-three soldiers from the Canadian army worked through the night on April 27 to repair a dike at a Manitoba farm. The contingent was part of a 6,000-person deployment of Canadian military fighting the flood. About 20,000 of the province's residents were evacuated from their homes.

BILL ALKOFER

AN ARMY OF HELP

Manitoba farmer Raymond Sabourin uses his tractor to transport Canadian Army troops on April 28 to his farm near St. Jean Baptiste that was in danger of being flooded. Soldiers from Princess Patricia's Canadian Light Infantry shored up Sabourin's dike.

BILL ALKOFER

FROM SUNRISE TO SUNSET (ABOVE)

Larry Kruse checks the condition of the dike in Drayton, N.D., at sunrise on April 22. Kruse, of St. Hilaire, Minn., volunteered as an equipment operator and was hired by the city to build dikes.

JOE ROSSI

A FIGHT FOR ALL FAITHS (LEFT)

Children from the Glenway Colony near Dominion City, Man., play near the Roseau River. People from the Mennonite and Hutterite faiths were active in the flood-relief efforts.

BILL ALKOFER

> ## *"We've lost everything. We have no money, no home,*
> ## *just ourselves and the clothes we're wearing."*

Bryan Satterwhite, East Grand Forks evacuee

A Rough First Day

At the end of his first day at his new school April 28, kindergartner Ricky Sonterre sits in the Thompson (N.D.) Public School office waiting for his mom to pick him up. Ricky and his family were evacuated from their Grand Forks home and found shelter with friends in Thompson. An estimated 11,000 students were displaced, with about 200 of them attending the Thompson School, increasing its enrollment by almost 40 percent.

Carolyn Kaster

A home on drier ground

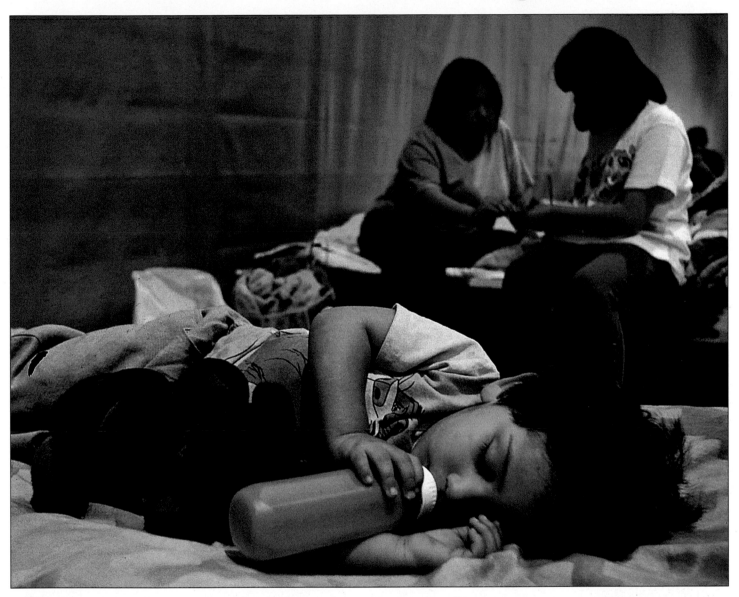

Diapers and baby formula. That's all Bryan Satterwhite and Rita Cook took with them when they fled East Grand Forks. And their 10-month-old son, Bryan Jr.

"We've lost everything," Satterwhite said from a cot in a Crookston shelter. "We have no money, no home, just ourselves and the clothes we're wearing."

Along with hundreds of others, the three were taken by bus to Crookston, where residents opened their community and their hearts to East Grand Forks residents who had nowhere to flee but east. Close to half the population of East Grand Forks — an estimated 4,000 suddenly homeless people — passed through Crookston's new high school. It was their first stop in search of shelter.

It was the first time the school was used. Its pristine hallways awaited the school's first students in the fall — but instead found mud-stained evacuees from 25 miles away. Evacuees found a fountain of generosity there.

Diane Wales of East Grand Forks was given a blanket, a cot, something to eat and some privacy to absorb her loss.

"They've just loved us, and that will help us to heal," Wales said, wiping

PEACEFUL REST IN SHELTER
Aaron Casiano, 2, sleeps in a shelter April 22 at the University of Minnesota-Crookston campus while his mother, Isabel Casiano, back and left, and aunt Suzie Casiano keep an eye on him. Crookston was the first stop for about 4,000 evacuees, most of them from East Grand Forks.

JUANITO HOLANDEZ

MAKING FRIENDS

Hazel Wilkinson, 81, talks with 2nd Lt. Matt Morand of the U.S. Air Force at the Red Cross shelter at Grand Forks Air Force Base.

JOE ROSSI

ALL DRESSED UP, NO PLACE TO GO

Steffie Benton fixes her hair the way she did before she was evacuated from her Oak Manor apartment. Benton was living with about 150 other flood refugees a month after the flood hit.

BEAU CABELL

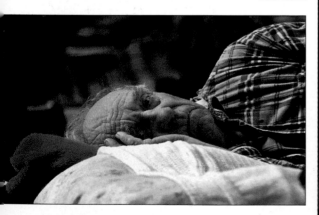

SLEEPLESS NIGHTS

Ed Wagner, 85, tries to fall asleep after a sleepless night in a Grand Forks Air Force Base shelter. Beds for more than 3,000 evacuees from the Red River Valley fill one of three F-16 fighter jet hangars, right, used for the displaced at Grand Forks Air Force Base.

JOSH MELTZER

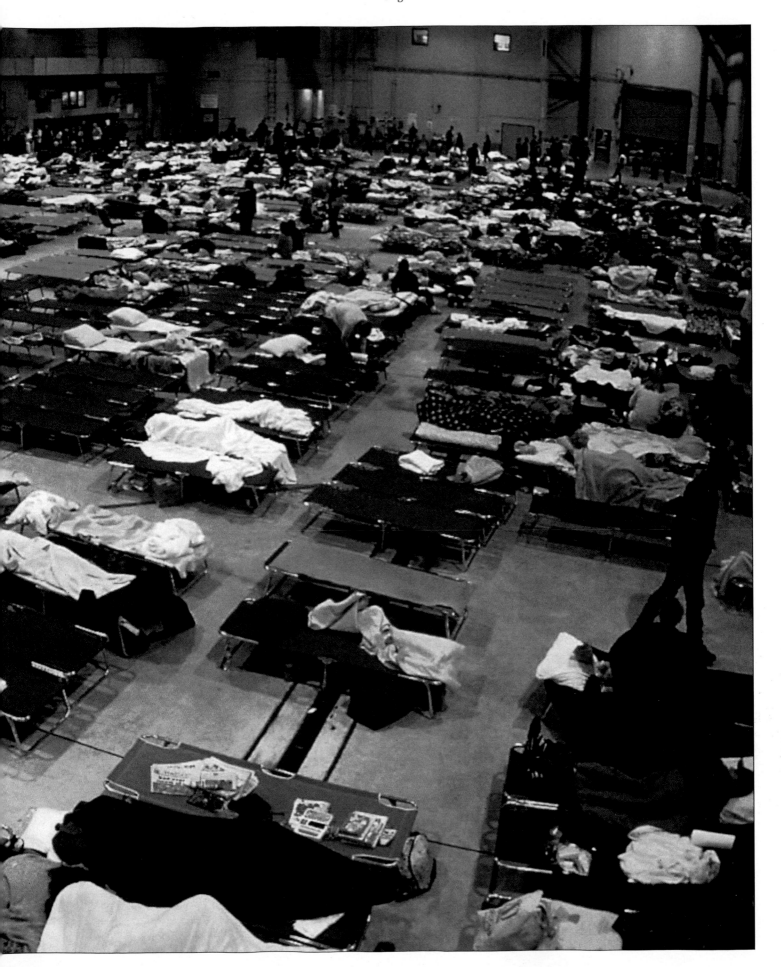

MAKING HIS NEW BED
(BELOW)
Five-year-old Christopher Convey makes his new bed in the shelter at Eagles Arena in Grand Forks. Evacuees living at Grand Forks Air Force Base were moved to Eagles Arena on May 7.

CANDACE BARBOT

RECREATION ON THE RESERVATION

Josh Nadeau, 11, left, from Belcourt, N.D., entertains guest Oscar Wilkie, 5, at the Turtle Mountain Reservation on April 24. Oscar and his mother, Tawn Wilkie, were among the 1,300 flood evacuees who found shelter at the reservation.

JUANITO HOLANDEZ

her eyes. "They say that one heart speaks to another heart, and I can hear it in the faces of people who say they're sorry."

It was like that everywhere. As more than 50,000 people from the sister cities sought haven, towns nearby — Thompson, Larimore, Manvel, Mayville and all the others — swelled to twice their normal size by taking in family, friends and even complete strangers. The evacuees — not refugees, they declared — found comfort wherever their escape took them. Mayville State University and UND-Lake Region in Devils Lake were needed so badly for relief help that officials canceled classes for the rest of the semester, and evacuees moved into students'

rooms.

Perhaps Crookston residents came closest to understanding the pain. They had waged a long fight of their own against the flooding Red Lake River. They were spared when the river crested below the top of their sandbag levees.

"It could have been us," Crookston volunteer Kris Derosier said. "I feel we've been blessed, and it's our turn to give."

Across the region, the story was the same. In Minneapolis and St. Paul, in Bemidji and Bismarck, in Fargo and Fosston, everywhere there was need, there were willing givers.

At Grand Forks Air Force Base, 3,000 people took shelter in three 175,000-square-foot hangars. Many had only

the clothes they were wearing; they left their homes that quickly.

It wasn't clothing, however, but telephones that were most desperately needed by evacuees, as husband sought wife and mother sought child. The calls were often frantic, voices laced with fear.

But they did find family. And they did find a home away from home, some for a day, some for weeks. Strangers around the region and around the country became neighbors.

In Crookston, Kathy Umlauf helped at the shelter. She said, "We keep saying to ourselves, 'Why did we get spared in this?' We think we've been spared to help."

A CHURCH IN EXILE (LEFT)
Erin Boese leans on her mom, Lyn Boese, during services of Faith Evangelical Free Church held at St. Matthew's Lutheran Church in Thompson, N.D.

ERIC HYLDEN

A FACE AT THE BASE (RIGHT)
Wallace "Wally" Dammen, 79, was among the evacuees at the Grand Forks Air Force Base shelter eight days after the flood.

JOHN STENNES

Receding water brings joy and sadness

When Deb Bidmead came home a week after the flood hit her house in Grand Forks, she found a basement full of water and a refrigerator full of rotting food. "It's wonderful," she said.

Wonderful because it could have been worse. Water could have reached the ground floor. With thousands of others, Bidmead happily assessed damage to her home: "Only the basement."

Throughout Grand Forks and East Grand Forks, residents dreaded and anticipated the return. They hoped for the best, and they feared the worst.

Whatever they found was met with tears, of either despair or relief.

Celia and Dennis Garland returned to their home on Walnut Street to find their brand-new 6-foot cedar fence in the neighbor's yard and water marks halfway up the outside of their home.

"I'm glad we got to see it," Dennis said from his yard. "I'd heard that the water was up to the roofs, so this isn't as bad as I thought. Mostly, I feel anxiety. Do I really want to go in there?"

He and others returning home found everything inside caked with mud and sewage, possessions now good for only the landfill. Coming home, residents first real-

THINKING ABOUT THEIR SON

Dennis and Sandy Dodge of Grand Forks stand on a dike two days before Mother's Day. They were missing their young son, who was living with his grandmother in another town.

CANDACE BARBOT

ized the extent of their personal and financial losses and the prospects of long cleanup.

Very few homes were spared basement damage, at least. Even those who were spared, such as Linda Dahl, couldn't bring themselves to be delighted.

"We're so thankful," Dahl said. "Then you start thinking about your friends, what they might be going through, and you feel guilty, remorseful."

The first homecomings were just afternoon visits of a few hours. Permanent returns had to wait for basement pumpings, electricians, power, inspectors, plumbers and more inspectors.

But few complained too loudly, realizing they could be residents of the neighborhoods where people found their homes ruined. Darlene Schroeder was one of them. She didn't find consolation in the inevitable buyout of her home in East Grand Forks' Sherlock Park.

"They can give me three houses, brand-new houses worth $300,000 each, and it's still not going to be my home," she said.

A WALK THROUGH THE PARK

East Grand Forks residents Stacy and Brad Hartze wade through waist-high waters as they return to their home in the Sherlock Park area for the first time on May 4. East Grand Forks residents were first allowed to visit their flooded homes on April 27, but hard-hit areas like Sherlock were opened later.

CANDACE BARBOT

MUDDY CUPBOARDS

Shelly Stewart mucks through rotten food and sludge in the kitchen of her sister's home on Polk Street on Mother's Day. The home in Lincoln Park took on water up to the attic.

CAROLYN KASTER

A LITTLE RUSTY

Wayne Kolstad of Grand Forks takes a break from his flood cleanup chores to air out his accordion on April 28.

JOHN STENNES

KNEE-DEEP IN DISBELIEF

George Cariveau looks down at nearly two feet of water in his son's basement bedroom on April 24, the first day Grand Forks residents were allowed back into their homes.

BILL ALKOFER

A SEA OF RUBBLE

Mike Zahradka checks on the basement of the home of friends Allen and Cathy Clement at 27th and Chestnut in Grand Forks.

BILL ALKOFER

"I'd probably be mowing the lawn today, but I don't have a lawn mower anymore. The flood took it away."

MARK BRODEN,
Grand Forks

A WET WARDROBE
Tara Johnson spreads clothes to dry on the lawn of her friend, Cindy Fetsch, in Grand Forks on May 2. They inventoried the clothes and washed the undamaged ones.
CHUCK KIMMERLE

"I've come to realize that the best things in life are not things."

THERESE SCHANILEC, Grand Forks

PORTABLE RELIEF

William Olson, 13, leaves a Porta-Potty in Grand Forks on April 29. Emergency officials set up more than 1,000 of the phone-booth-sized bathrooms in Grand Forks.

RICHARD WISDOM

A TEARFUL BOOK OF MEMORIES

Therese Schanilec cries as she looks through her memory book in her flooded basement apartment in Grand Forks on April 25.

BILL ALKOFER

"We're so thankful. Then you start thinking about your friends, what they might be going through, and you feel guilty, remorseful."

LINDA DAHL, East Grand Forks

PLEASE READ THE SIGN
(NEXT PAGE)
Paul Fredrickson steps through the door of a friend's house in the Sherlock Park neighborhood of East Grand Forks on May 11. Another family friend used mud to paint the greeting.

CHUCK KIMMERLE

OFF THE FOUNDATION
Don Devos, right, stands on the deck of his dislodged house in the Lincoln Drive area and points out the destruction to his sister Marian and her husband, Chuck Suda. Floodwaters lifted Devos' house off its foundation and dropped it on the hood of his car.

JOHN STENNES

Mud, sweat and tears

Here's a number that tells the story of the magnitude of the post-flood cleanup. Debris removed from homes in Grand Forks and East Grand Forks and trucked to the landfills totaled 112,000 tons. That's 224 million pounds.

But that tonnage — normally nine months' worth of garbage — doesn't do justice to the massive work and heartache that went into gutting, ripping, hauling, piling, hosing, scrubbing and disinfecting.

Plus, things that weighed the least meant the most.

"It's the little things you think about," Lori Laturnus said as she held a soaked videotape of a family vacation.

Little things like family scrapbooks and photo albums were the heaviest to carry to the berms. "I never thought to. . ." Roxanne Miller said through tears as she discovered a box of high school yearbooks and old photographs.

The water went away, but the destruction and grime remained and had to be dealt with. Seeing the flood's residue was more difficult than seeing homes surrounded by water. The devastation was hidden then.

The only possessions salvageable from Jeff LaFrenz's recently remodeled three-bedroom home were dishes, a lawn mower and bicycles.

"Every time you come

WRINGING OUT MEMORIES
Gordon Gronhovd holds up a flood-soaked print from the day in 1948 when he married his wife, Dee. The photograph is one of thousands salvaged from Gronhovd's basement darkroom on Belmont Road.

ERIC HYLDEN

"It was pretty much everything I expected, but worse."

DANIEL DAMICO,
Concordia College student from East Grand Forks

here, it's hard," he said. "My wife won't come anymore. It's tough for me to leave. It's almost like ending a book that you don't want to end."

Mud and sweat mingled with tears as residents worked to bring their homes to livability. It was a dirty job, and almost everyone had to do it. Mud was everywhere, often accompanied by sewage or fuel oil,

---

"Where do we start? Where do we start?... Everything you worked for — for 50 years — and what's it all for?"

MILDRED RUDRUD,
Grand Forks

---

forming a caustic brew.

Pumping came first. Then the heavy lifting of furniture, appliances and furnaces. Next the Sheetrock, paneling and carpets were pulled up. Finally — and worst of all — everything had to be scrubbed with chlorine bleach.

The ordeal didn't end after the weeks of cleanup. After gutting houses, residents had to look at their pasts sitting

in heaps on the curb, some for as long as six weeks.

"You shut your eyes and throw it out," Gary Schill said after his pile headed to the landfill. "It was part of your life, but it's so good not to have to look at it anymore.

"Once it's gone, you can take that first step toward feeling you can go on."

Going on got easier — because of the volunteers who came from near and far. Strangers joined family and friends to help with the cleanup. Students came from the campus of Texas A&M University in Corpus Christi. Firefighters came from Halifax, Va. Wilkes Barre, Pa., sent a busload of volunteers, all of whom had experience with their own flood. Inmates from the Stillwater State Prison in Minnesota came. A Baptist youth group came from Missouri. Mennonite Brethren teen-agers came from Kansas. Volunteers from the Red Cross and the Salvation Army came from all around the country.

And there were many more.

Some came unattached and unannounced, going door to door, simply offering help. They were not unappreciated. With the strength of their families, the help of their friends and the kindness of strangers, the devastated cities began to rebuild.

A PUSH TOWARD RECOVERY

Sherlock Park residents Dave Sandahl, left, Dan Sandahl and David Corneillie flip a camper upright on May 5. The custom-made camper, weighing 700 pounds, was carried more than 100 yards from their home by the water.

CANDACE BARBOT

WALL-TO-WALL MUCK (ABOVE)

Jeremy Swanson of Opp Construction uses a power washer in the basement of the City Center Mall in Grand Forks.

ERIC HYLDEN

COMMANDOS OF COMMUNICATION (RIGHT)

US West technician Jeff Shearer splices broken lines in the cable vault at US West's downtown Grand Forks building. Employees worked nonstop to maintain service to 60,000 customers in 17 communities.

CHUCK KIMMERLE

DOWN AND FLOODED OUT
Lincoln Drive resident A.B. Dickie pauses for a reflective moment on his front steps as he and friends salvage what's left of his belongings in his flooded home on May 21.

ERIC HYLDEN

BELONGINGS ON THE BERMS

Piles of flood-soaked belongings line the 2700 block of Cherry Street on May 5. After six weeks of collecting the flood debris in the two cities, 224 million pounds had been removed from the berms.

CHUCK KIMMERLE

GETTING RID OF THE REFUSE

A line of dump trucks empties loads of flood debris on May 16 at the Grand Forks Landfill just off of U.S. Highway 2 west of Grand Forks. When the debris pickup operation hit full stride, 120 trucks carried about 6 million pounds a day to the landfill.

CHUCK KIMMERLE

FREEZING TIME

A photograph is rinsed with water on May 7 before being frozen to prevent mold. The process allowed the Grand Forks County Historical Society to restore the documents.

JACKIE LORENTZ

DRENCHED DOLLS

Nicole Meyer's doll collection dries on the clothesline on April 28 after getting soaked in the basement of her University Avenue residence in Grand Forks.

JOHN STENNES

A Helping Hand

Displaced flood victims line up outside South Forks Plaza to receive food distributed by the Salvation Army.

Meri Simon

Bridge of Troubled Water

Dried mud cracks on the Sorlie Bridge on May 2. The bridge, which links the downtowns of Grand Forks and East Grand Forks, reopened May 13, almost a month after high water forced its closing.

Juanito Holandez

A GUARDIAN FROM ABOVE

A velvet wall hanging of Jesus hangs above a pile of debris along a berm in the Lincoln Park area. Looting and scavenging were held to a minimum because of extra law enforcement officers and watchful neighbors.

BILL ALKOFER

RESUSCITATING ANNE

YMCA Family Center Executive Director Dave Snow, right, and Aquatic Director Tom Saari look over the flood-damaged Resusci Anne and other CPR practice dummies on May 24. The YMCA Family Center suffered an estimated $1 million in damage.

JACKIE LORENTZ

HUMOR IN THE DISASTER

A mannequin placed in an abandoned convertible provides some much-needed humor for residents on April 30.

J. ALBERT DIAZ

CHURCH'S CLEARINGHOUSE
Lori Hein dumps a flood-soaked roll of carpet onto the garbage pile in front of Zion United Methodist Church on May 2. The church had six feet of water in the basement.

CHUCK KIMMERLE

HER PRICELESS PIANO
Grand Forks resident Inga Koppang mourns the loss of her piano on May 1.

RICHARD WISDOM

A SURVIVOR SMILES (LEFT)
Kelly Straub seeks to retain her balance as she walks across the furniture strewn around the living room of her Lincoln Park home.

ERIC HYLDEN

BYE BYE BOOTS
Ten pairs of muddy boots wait for curbside trash pickup.

CANDACE BARBOT

Flooding fills our homes; faith brings us back

On April 22, President Clinton landed in Grand Forks, offering encouragement and promising millions of dollars in federal help.

"You bring us hope," Grand Forks Mayor Pat Owens told Clinton as she wiped away a tear.

On April 29, an angel landed, delivering $15 million in $2,000 allotments and more hope.

"Two thousand dollars is a lot right now. It seems like $100,000," said Cindy Janisch of East Grand Forks. East Grand Forks Mayor Lynn Stauss described the gift as "a ray of sunshine."

Angel, later identified as McDonald's heiress Joan Kroc, certainly helped recovery by fattening thin wallets and lifting sagging spirits. The federal money, not coming for another two months, was a comfort in both ways, too.

But recovery didn't start when Angel landed or when Clinton arrived. It began when the first

MOTHER'S DAY PRESENT
Wearing a swimming suit that her children gave her as an early Mother's Day present, Kelly Straub, center, cleans "all the possessions we have left." Daughters Molly, 13, and Emily, 11, and son Andrew, 8, help wash glass and silverware on May 10.

BEAU CABELL

"Our lives have been dumped in a heap in the middle of the street, to be piled in a truck and taken away."

Lori Stennes, Grand Forks

UP AND AT 'EM

Kim Goninan and Heather Lueck wake up and prepare for work on May 3. The two Wal-Mart employees, on loan from Baxter, Minn., stayed in a recreational vehicle stationed at the Grand Forks Wal-Mart parking lot.

MERI SIMON

Greater Grand Forks residents landed back at their flooded homes, eyed the daunting task ahead, accepted the challenge and refused to surrender.

Residents such as Jay and Jennifer Knutson of East Grand Forks.

Their small yellow Victorian home took knee-deep water on the first floor, muddying the carpet, weakening walls, buckling floors and destroying Jennifer's wedding dress and grandma's antique table, among other possessions.

"We were pretty proud of this place," Jay said.

Proud because they'd remodeled almost every room of the house they would have owned after six more years of mortgage payments.

"I'm fairly upbeat," Jay said. "Maybe it's the Norwegian in me. But I know we'll rebuild — somewhere.

"It's a setback. Now we'll have to buy another house and have bigger house payments, probably for another 30 years. But we're trying to stay positive. We have to."

They have to because they want their two children to grow up in East Grand Forks, where Jay was born and raised.

And no river was going to change those plans.

Jay, Jennifer and thousands of other flood victims in the region had a sea of help in recovering from the river.

KEEPING KITTY COZY

Amber Vaughn keeps her kitten, Tigger, warm while she waits to be interviewed as a potential guest on the "Oprah Winfrey Show." Vaughn wasn't chosen.

ERIC HYLDEN

The Salvation Army became more than a kettle. The American Red Cross became more than CPR classes. The National Guard became more than "Weekend Warriors." The Army Corps of Engineers and FEMA became people, not uncaring, bureaucratic agencies.

College and high school students, Air Force personnel and residents of high ground became volunteers in the cleanup brigades, just as they'd been links in the sandbagging chains a week earlier.

Leaders led the way, in word and deed. Owens, the plucky spitfire, showed her compassion through her tears and her strength through the grit of words that were so inspiring that grizzled reporters broke into applause.

Stauss wore his loyalty to country and city on his sweatshirts and never was too busy to talk to an East Sider. "I'm a mayor without a city," he said. So the mayor went to his city, traveling to Bemidji, Warren, Crookston and elsewhere to reconnect with his scattered populace.

The news media became a lifeline. The Grand Forks Herald showed that all was possible by not missing an edition despite fire and flood, giving evacuees a part of their city that they could hold in their hands. WDAZ-TV helped family members find each other and evacuees find shelter. KCNN, KFJM and KNOX radio stations provided news' immediacy and around-the-clock answers during call-in shows.

Signs of recovery, of normalcy, came daily, in small but significant ways. The Kennedy Bridge reopened, providing a physi-

FAITH IN FATIGUES

Chaplain Steve Anderson's camouflage Bible sits on his makeshift altar during a service.

JOHN STENNES

A PRAYER OF HOPE

Bismarck police chaplain Terry Kern prays with the Faith Evangelical Free Church congregation in Thompson, N.D.

ERIC HYLDEN

A BLESSING FROM THE BISHOP

The Rev. Steve Riske follows as Bishop James Sullivan blesses a new day-care facility on May 6. The facility was established by area Catholics to provide free day-care service for the community.

JACKIE LORENTZ

cal link between the cities linked by catastrophe. Drinkable water was restored. Power came back. So did home mail service. Porcelain replaced Porta-Potties. Restaurants reopened. Marilyn Hagerty's column returned. So did United Hospital, and our favorite stores, restaurants and taverns.

Some things were gone, such as Mayor Pat's gavel. She used a can of purified water to open the first City Council meeting after the flood.

Also gone in the sister cities was upward of $300 million of personal property. There was $800 million of damage to residential and commercial buildings, according to Federal Reserve Bank estimates.

Not gone are the likes of Jay and Jennifer Knutson, and thousands of others, all muddied but unbroken. They, not the buildings and the water heaters, are Grand Forks and East Grand Forks.

"When the water started going down, our spirits went up."

RENAE LESTER,
Burke Addition resident

REINFORCEMENTS ARRIVE (ABOVE)

The first flight of 250 volunteers from the Twin Cities arrives at the Grand Forks International Airport May 10. Northwest Airlines provided free transportation for this group as well as another group of 250 volunteers from the Twin Cities.

JOHN STENNES

FLY-BY WITH A SMILE

The Northern Lights Aerobatic Team spreads some joy in the skies over Grand Forks on May 27 with their air show.

ERIC HYLDEN

*"Believe me, it may be hard to believe it now,
but you can rebuild stronger
and better than ever."*

BILL CLINTON,
president of the United States
on his April 22 visit

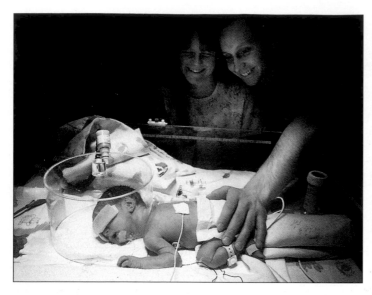

A NEW CITY'S FIRST NEWBORN

Wanda and Shane Leske reach out for their baby, Josiah, born May 12 at United Hospital. Josiah, who was in the neonatal intensive care unit because he was born seven weeks early, was the first baby born at United in the post-flood era.

ERIC HYLDEN

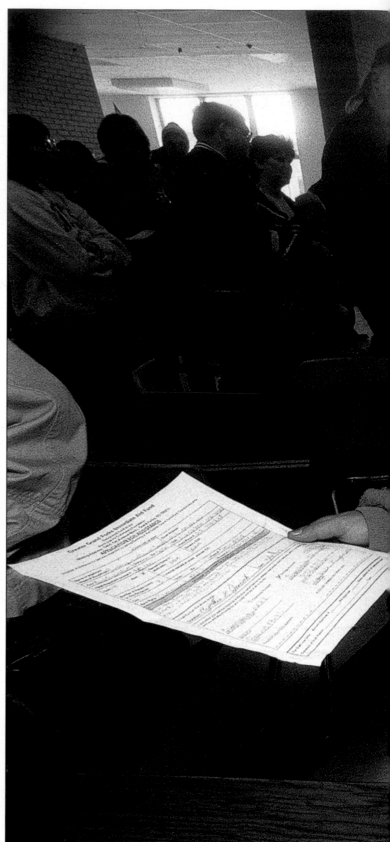

FROM ONE DISASTER TO ANOTHER

American Red Cross veteran volunteer Bob Underhill takes a call from his motel room office. Underhill, from Osprey, Fla., was among 849 Red Cross volunteers who had come from across the country to help the valley's recovery by April 30. Many more followed.

JUANITO HOLANDEZ

GETTING THE GIFT

Cindy Janisch, 26, and daughter Ariel, 3, move through a line at East Grand Forks Senior High April 30 for the $2,000 checks from the Angel Fund that were given to Greater Grand Forks flood victims. Joan Kroc's $15 million donation was followed by a $5 million donation from the Ronald McDonald House Foundation.

JOHN DOMAN

Democracy gets messy after the flood

Democracy can be a dirty business, flood-weary residents of Grand Forks and East Grand Forks discovered.

No sooner had the waters receded than the cities were flooded by government agents — from FEMA (Federal Emergency Management Agency), SBA (Small Business Administration), NFIP (National Flood Insurance Program), HUD (Housing and Urban Development Department) and the Corps (U.S. Army Corps of Engineers). Then the hard part started.

City governments faced difficult decisions about how to proceed with buyouts of flood-damaged houses, whether to build a dike or a ditch to protect the cities from future floods, whether to grant building permits in flood-prone areas, whether to relax the rules governing new developments.

Occasionally, the people became impatient. "Make a decision," a frustrated homeowner yelled at Grand Forks City Council members during a marathon meeting.

On the whole, however. Greater Grand Forks reacted to the flood of bureaucracy much as they had reacted to the river's own flood, with stoic good humor. Rebuilding the town, it turned out, would be a long, hard job. And so we put our shoulders to it.

MANY QUESTIONS
Gary Decker of Grand Forks raises a point at a public meeting about flood control alternatives. Waiting to speak are Geri Alberts (center) and Gayle Clifford.

JOHN STENNES

TWO SIDES

John Dickinson has a heavy discussion with Grand Forks City Council member Ann Sande during a neighborhood meeting on June 12. Dickinson's house is on Walnut Place, an area hard hit by floodwaters.

ERIC HYLDEN

Grand Forks City Council member Ken Polovitz listens to debate at the June 6 City Council meeting.

JOHN STENNES

DESIRE FOR DECISIONS

A crowd of nearly 1,100 concerned residents filled the first floor of the Chester Fritz Auditorium on May 12 at the second Grand Forks City Council meeting after the flood. Angry residents pleaded for the council to make a decision about a flood-protection plan.

ERIC HYLDEN

The night to remember

It was the prom of the century.

That's how 18-year-old Chris Cates described the combined Red River, Central and Community high school prom on June 28.

It started with Bob Rost in the Grand Forks County Sheriff's Office. The teens deserved a reward for the sweat and tears they spent trying to fend off the flood; he thought he'd try to land a big-name band to play their prom.

Enter North Carolina philanthropist Marie Wilber-Carr, who, through contacts within the American Society of Composers, Artists and Publishers, rounded up Grammy Award-winning rock band Soul Asylum. The band agreed to make the trip for free.

On June 28, in the spotlight of national media, the stars arrived, more than 1,200 of them, all dressed to kill but prepared to shine. They came to dance, to celebrate and to bring closure to a school year aborted by disaster.

Echoing the words of Grand Forks Mayor Pat Owens, 17-year-old Amy Silletto reflected the emotions taking root throughout the wounded city:

"We'll come back better than ever."

DANCING THE NIGHT AWAY
(PREVIOUS PAGE)

Master Sgt. Steve Miller, Airman Jonathan Meyer and Master Sgt. James Blackmun raise the flag before the prom. (TOP)

CAROLYN KASTER

Nicky Marden watches her mom, Phyllis Marden, pin flowers on Marc Fetsch before the prom. Marc lost his tuxedo and Nicky her prom dress in the flood. Marc choose to go casual; Nicky wore a donated dress. (CENTER, LEFT)

CAROLYN KASTER

Aleece Whitcomb prepares for the prom. (CENTER, RIGHT, TOP)

CAROLYN KASTER

The military and the media watch as promgoers arrive at Grand Forks Air Force Base. (CENTER, RIGHT, BOTTOM)

CHUCK KIMMERLE

Cols. Mike Collings and Mickey Melton remain alert as Brandi Frederick and Shilo Boese dance. (BOTTOM)

CAROLYN KASTER

NIGHTS TO REMEMBER

Students dance at the East Grand Forks Senior High School prom, held on schedule in May. (ABOVE)

JOHN STENNES

Couples arriving at the Grand Forks prom pass under the drawn swords of a U.S. Air Force honor guard. (BELOW)

CAROLYN KASTER

SLOW DANCING
Ann Cape and Matt Johnson dance at the prom.
CAROLYN KASTER

FORGETTING THE FLOOD
A sandbag became a decoration for the 1997 prom at Grand Forks Air Force Base. The music of Soul Asylum, a Grammy award-winning rock band, helped students forget the flood that disrupted plans for their prom.
BILL ALKOFER

Come hell and high water, the Herald delivers

The Grand Forks Herald lost two of its three buildings in the fire that struck downtown Grand Forks on April 19.

But the newspaper did not miss an issue.

The University of North Dakota provided computers enough for the Herald staff to produce an issue on the first day of the flood. When the university was overwhelmed by floodwaters, the Herald moved to the public school in Manvel, N.D., where Principal Richard Ray welcomed the staff, and Vicki Leiberg, the school cook, furnished warm cookies and cold milk.

Each day, Herald editors planned coverage that would show in graphic detail what had happened in Grand Forks, East Grand Forks and the region. Each day, reporters and photographers went out to report on flooded areas, sometimes including their own homes and their own workplace. And each day, the Herald circulation staff sent the newspapers to evacuation shelters throughout the region. So that each day, flood victims had something that came from Grand Forks.

The help of a major media corporation made it easier to produce the Herald every day. Knight-Ridder Inc. owns the Herald. Herald staff went to the newsroom of the St. Paul Pioneer Press,

another Knight-Ridder paper, and produced pages there. For almost a month, the Herald was printed in St. Paul. Journalists came from other Knight-Ridder newspapers to help report on the flood. Knight-Ridder sent help for other Herald departments. It even sent cash to pay Herald employees.

Flood and fire changed the Herald, bringing its staff a clearer understanding of the importance of the newspaper in the community. Editor Mike Jacobs described the relationship as "first-person plural. Now we use the word 'we' to mean 'we who live here' as opposed to its old meaning in the newspaper of 'we who know what is good for you, the readers.' "

Publisher Mike Maidenberg explained to the graduating class of Columbia University, his alma mater:

"Water washes away all that is nonessential.

"Flames burn away all that is superficial.

"What remains is a core, which, if strong and true, stands as a rock despite flood and fire. ...

"We have been given a forceful lesson in how

TIME STANDS STILL

The last issue of the Grand Forks Herald to be printed from the downtown location remains threaded through the presses that shut down at 2:20 a.m. April 19. At that time, employees had to evacuate because water was rushing down the alley. About 9,500 of a scheduled run of 44,000 newspapers were printed before the presses stopped.

JACKIE LORENTZ

SIGN OF HOPE

(PREVIOUS PAGES)

A rainbow appears over the fire-ravaged First National Bank building as the sun sets in downtown Grand Forks on April 28.

J. ALBERT DIAZ

A TEMPORARY NEWSROOM IN MANVEL
Herald Editor Mike Jacobs talks about issues of the day in the computer room of the Manvel (N.D.) Public School. The Herald published from Manvel for 71 days after the flood and fire that drove them from their downtown building.

GEORGE SCHIAVONE

fundamental a newspaper is in the media ecosystem. We do not have radio's immediacy, nor television's visual impact, nor online's depth and detail, but our readers have told us, passionately, that our role is to set the framework, to undergird all other media, to provide a sense of shared community, because only a newspaper can create a tangible, comprehensive, authoritative, enduring version of the news.

"This is our core as a news medium, and it flows out of the irreducible values we at the Herald hold as individuals.

"We are a newspaper. What we do is publish. We have a covenant with our readers that we will

not break, come hell and high water.

"When all else is stripped away, this is the value that remains at our core."

WE CONTINUE TO PUBLISH
Rubble from the Herald's burned-out building surrounds a vending machine containing the April 18 issue, the last to be distributed from the Herald's downtown building.

GEORGE SCHIAVONE

We got by with help from our friends

None of this would be possible except for the people who put out the Grand Forks Herald, "come hell and high water."

Those who worked on the book were:

Ryan Bakken
writer

Dan Diedrich
photographer

Greg Harmel
artist

Lee Hulteng
artist

Eric Hylden
photographer

Mike Jacobs
editor

Kris Jensen
copy editor

Chuck Kimmerle
photographer

Jackie Lorentz
photographer

Erik Siemers
research

Jenelle Stadstad
support

John Stennes
chief photographer

They drew on the work of the Herald's newsroom staff and the support of Herald Publisher Michael Maidenberg and Herald employees and carriers who deliver the newspaper.

Special thanks to reporters, photographers, editors and others who came from more than 20 Knight-Ridder newspapers.

Work by these people appears in this book:

Bill Alkofer
St. Paul Pioneer Press

Candace Barbot
Miami Herald

Beau Cabell
Macon Telegraph

J. Albert Diaz
Miami Herald

John Doman
St. Paul Pioneer Press

David P. Gilkey
Detroit Free Press

Elizabeth Hefelfinger
Tallahassee Democrat

Juanito Holandez
Long Beach Press Telegram

Randy Johnson
St. Paul Pioneer Press

Carolyn Kaster
St. Paul Pioneer Press

Josh Meltzer
Duluth News-Tribune

Joe Rossi
St. Paul Pioneer Press

Jeff Rush
St. Paul Pioneer Press

George Schiavone
Knight-Ridder News

Meri Simon
San Jose Mercury News

Scott Takushi
St. Paul Pioneer Press

Richard Wisdom
San Jose Mercury News

Extra special thanks to editor/designer Steve Rice of Seattle, and to Dave Bacig and Mike Bulger of the St. Paul Pioneer Press for technical help.

Thanks to Peter Ridder, publisher, and Walker Lundy, editor, and to the people of the Pioneer Press who helped make it possible to publish the Herald every day.

Thanks to Tony Ridder, president and chief executive officer of Knight-Ridder Inc., for his swift and caring response to our emergency. Thanks to members of Knight-Ridder's corporate staff, who provided many kinds of support, and especially to Marty Claus, Willie Cone, Woody Helfand, Mindi Keirnan, Frank McDonald, Jane Sutter and Bill Wilson.

Thanks to the University of North Dakota, Kendall Baker, president, for offering work space to the Herald — until the flood forced us out.

We also want to thank the Manvel Public School, Richard Ray, principal, Trinity Lutheran Church and the people of Manvel, N.D., for their extraordinary generosity in giving the Herald a home. They showed us that our many towns are one community.

And thanks to the people of Grand Forks and East Grand Forks, who are working together in the wake of the flood to make our community bigger, better and stronger.

Thanks also to the thousands of volunteers who came to Greater Grand Forks, adding the kindness of strangers to the help of our friends. Their efforts will never be forgotten.